THIS
IS NOT
WHO
I AM

Emily Bootle

THIS IS NOT WHO I AM

Our Authenticity Obsession

ORTAC PRESS

The right of Emily Bootle to be identified as the author of this work has been
asserted by her in accordance with the Copyright, Designs and Patents Act 1988.

The best effort has been made to contact the copyright holders of material
reproduced in this book prior to publication and obtain permissions where necessary.
If required, we the publishers are happy to make restitutions at a later date.

While care has been taken to ensure that the web links in the Notes Section
are accurate at the time of publication, the publisher cannot guarantee
that these links remain viable. The author and publisher assume no
responsibility for the content of websites that are not their own.

First published in Great Britain in 2022 by Ortac Press

ISBN: 978-1-8383887-3-7

A CIP record for this book is available from the British Library

Cover design by Jo Walker

Typeset in Monotype Dante by Tetragon, London
Printed and bound by by CPI Group (UK) Ltd, Croydon, CRO 4YY

ortacpress.com

For my parents

CONTENTS

INTRODUCTION

Authenticity is such a familiar idea in contemporary culture that it can feel as though aspiring to it is some innate human instinct. However, it has not always existed as a concept. Its significance has steadily grown since it emerged in the late 1700s. Now, in the West, it is everywhere: not only reassuring buyers of second-hand designer bags or art of their genuineness, but invoked in A-list celebrity profiles, printed on socks from H&M, weaponised in populist politics and, most of all, burned on to our minds as a steadfast goal for life.

It can be tempting simply to accept its prevalence – it would be possible, in fact, not to notice it at all. Authenticity is highly convenient. It provides purpose and, in its demand for introspection, some semblance of spirituality in our secular society. It justifies focusing on the pursuit of individual happiness rather than any more difficult, collective aim (though it should be said that many people pursue self-authenticity so that they are better equipped to help the collective). In writing this book, I am setting out to question the mandate to be authentic, which in its present iteration is, in my view, not always as helpful as it appears.

Before authenticity, the definition of which we'll come to shortly, there was sincerity. The distinction between the two is considered in detail in Lionel Trilling's *Sincerity and Authenticity*,[1] which I have drawn on in parts of this book. It offers a thorough account of the evolution of the two concepts throughout literature. The doctrine of sincerity that guided life in the seventeenth and eighteenth centuries meant that you should – as Polonius tells Laertes in *Hamlet* – 'to thine own self be true'[2] so that the structure of society was maintained. To be sincere was not so much to 'live your truth' as we now conceive it, but rather to be honest – the aim was to avoid deceiving other people, not yourself. Who you were was as bound up in your social status, rank, job or other societal position as any innate personality or essence. There was no sense that the fulfilment of the individual as a distinct entity was a goal in itself.

Authenticity arose in the late eighteenth century as part of a budding Romanticism, an artistic movement that prized individual self-expression. The foundational idea of authenticity is that a unique, true self exists within each of us – a 'real me' that is separate from all the things that are not the real me.[3] Being authentic was in many ways in opposition to being sincere. It meant actively overthrowing societal structures or circumstances – anything not intrinsic to the individual soul – to liberate the true, inner self and let it reign. Etymologically, authenticity derives from the Greek *auto*, meaning self, one's own, or of itself. It speaks to something organic and contained; as Charles Guignon put it in *On Being Authentic*, it is 'an ideal of *owning* oneself, of achieving *self-possession*'.[4] Guignon's definition takes on heightened significance when we consider the contemporary idea of the 'personal brand', which takes 'owning oneself' to an extreme.

The thinker most commonly associated with the emergence of authenticity – and Romanticism – is Jean-Jacques Rousseau (1712–1778), who considered that it was society and its rules causing unhappiness and that humanity should return to a natural, organic state. He committed to a project of self-documentation – his *Confessions*[5] – that would be comprehensive enough to fully convey the essence of who he was. Rousseau believed that to be authentic (though he did not actually use the word) you must not only *be* who you are but be *seen* to be who you are. Others must recognise you in the same way that you recognise yourself – an idea which is strikingly pertinent more than two centuries later in the age of social media.

In the early twentieth century, Sigmund Freud and other early psychoanalysts sought to help patients understand their hidden inner self so they could live a more fulfilling life. In the decades that followed the existentialists explored authenticity, too: Jean Paul Sartre, for example, wrote that by play-acting your role too well in a given context, you limit your freedom as an individual. Throughout the twentieth century, authenticity became embedded in society. It now serves as a moral bolster for the individualism that drives capitalism, and has for decades been sold back to us as a desirable – yet difficult to pin down – characteristic of commodities.

Today, authenticity has several meanings, often used loosely and interchangeably in common parlance. The meaning is usually instinctive in context – which is why I have used the word relatively freely in this book – but, for the avoidance of doubt, here are the variations. The first meaning speaks to the authenticity of an object: its genuineness; its being what it says it is. The second is a qualitative authenticity: this is when we use 'authentic' as a synonym for rustic, organic or relatable. The third, and most important to this book, is authenticity of self: the idea that each person has a distinct inner self that should be realised and a truth that should be lived. Though I remain sceptical about whether authenticity is a genuinely meaningful concept, for the sake of readability and open-mindedness I have also used the word as it is commonly used rather than questioning it at every possible juncture.

Given that authenticity exists in opposition to something – the external forces pushing or pulling you in a different direction from your true self – its contemporary prevalence is unsurprising. Arguably, we need authenticity of the first definition more than ever: social media – and the internet more broadly – has given us enormous scope for fakery and dishonesty, giving rise to what is often described as a 'post-truth' society. It has also provided us with the means to have our authentic self (in the context of the third definition) recognised by others through online engagement (which, as I explore, tends to be possible through deployment of the second definition). That corporations have seized the authenticity agenda for their own gain does not mean that it does not still serve as a conceptual antidote to the hyper-capitalism that has consumed Western culture: tapping into some sense of inner self can protect us from being engulfed by work.

I am not a philosopher or an academic, so I have not attempted to situate this book in the context of Rousseau, Sartre or any other canonical philosophy. I am also not trying to put this into an Eastern philosophical context, where there is extensive thought on the nature of self. For a comprehensive overview of the history of authenticity, I recommend Guignon's book *On Being Authentic*; Trilling's *Sincerity and Authenticity* for a literary perspective; and Charles Taylor's *The Ethics of Authenticity*[6] for a relatively modern interrogation of the concept. The perspective I hope to offer is contemporary cultural commentary: I have attempted to show and interrogate the seemingly unending ways in which authenticity has infiltrated our lives today.

Because it grapples with events and perceptions rather than concepts and ideas per se, including those that occur online, this book can only ever be a snapshot. I cannot be – as Rousseau might have wished – entirely comprehensive. In the two years that I have been working on the book, the landscape has shifted, subtly but tangibly. 'Authenticity' is less fashionable as a word as it has slipped into overuse. That this is the case only proves that it is impossible to sustain its meaning in a wider context and that, as a *concept*, it is both more apt and more contradictory than ever. Authenticity is about escaping societal circumstances and doctrines, but now to be authentic *is* the rule to be escaped. This may mean that the markers of authenticity begin to look different – as they undoubtedly have for Gen Z online – but the more claustrophobic society's rules become, the more significance it takes on as an idea. Similarly, authenticity has lost its meaning as it has become subsumed by capitalism – which ironically only increases the appeal of products that profess to help make you less conformist and beholden to a traditional view of success, and instead simply more 'yourself'.

Although I have attempted to critique and probe authenticity culture, this book is not an attack on the people beholden to it, especially not people who try to harness it for good. I am not exempt: many of the ideas in this book have naturally sprung from my own struggles with the nature of selfhood and happiness. The advocation of authenticity has undoubtedly also been a force for positive change, giving voice to communities previously silenced and giving purpose to those often penned in by societal expectations.

Where I have discussed identity I have not, for reasons that become clear in the essay in question, signposted my own: I have taken note in particular of the ideas in Emma Dabiri's 2021 book *What White People Can Do Next*,[7] in which she considers that sometimes acknowledging one's own 'privilege' entrenches that external identity as part of the self; the conflation of these two things is, I argue, one of the primary problems in the present 'culture wars'. I will say here, then, for the avoidance of doubt, simply that I am not claiming to understand fully or attempting to impinge upon the experience of the identity groups I have mentioned or the individuals within them.

This book is structured broadly in three sections – culture, politics and self – each comprising two essays. I have attempted to analyse what I perceive to be the most clear-cut examples of authenticity culture and identify the areas in which it ties itself in knots or causes more problems than it alleviates. The paradox of authenticity is that it is supposed to be about freedom – but when it becomes doctrine, that freedom is taken away. So while it is clearly a good thing that we *can* 'live our truth', I challenge the idea that we must.

Most importantly, I invite you to question any sense of anxiety you may have that you are not presently 'authentic'; that one life could be more 'real' than another; or that our 'truth' is anything beyond precisely what is happening right now, in this exact moment, when- and wherever you – whoever you may be – are reading this.

CELEBRITY

The existence of celebrities, as the film studies professor Richard Dyer wrote in his 1979 book *Stars*, has always depended on their being both ordinary and extraordinary, present and absent.[1] They must be enough like us that we feel an affinity with them, yet sufficiently unlike us that we worship them, too. They must remain in our field of vision yet be far away enough that we have to squint for a better look. Their success, however expansive, is a result of both democracy and luck. Somewhere down the line they had their big break, but the continuation of their fame is never guaranteed – it must be constantly fuelled by the attention of critics and fans. When we behold the celebrity spectacle, we need to think on some level that it could be us in their position, but also feel deeply that it isn't. And for the relationship between celebrities and the public to work, there must also be faith: we believe them, believe in them, believe that they somehow deserve their riches and privileges. Celebrity culture is a collision of the illusive and the authentic.

Such deep contradictions naturally create problems both ontological and practical. The sociologist Francesco Alberoni wrote in 1972 that celebrities are a 'powerless elite'.[2] Celebrity status is derived from their popularity, and popularity depends on the whims of the public, which means the celebrity landscape naturally shifts with societal preferences. So while in their popularity celebrities can appear to be leading the pack, they are also simply vessels into which the public can pour their desires.

Much early analysis of celebrity culture categorised it as shallow and vacuous, a facet of the mass culture propping up capitalism. 'Being a star means specialising in the seemingly lived; the star is the object of identification with the shallow seeming life that has to compensate for the fragmented productive specialisations which are actually lived', wrote Guy Debord in *Society of the Spectacle*.[3] In *The Image* the historian Daniel Boorstin described celebrities as 'human pseudo-events' who have replaced – and whose proliferation has diluted the essence of – true heroes. 'The celebrity is a person who is known for his well-knownness,' Boorstin wrote. 'He has been fabricated on purpose to satisfy our exaggerated expectations of human greatness… He is made by all of us who willingly read about him, who like to see him on television, who buy recordings of his voice, and talk about him to our friends. His relation to… reality is highly ambiguous.'[4]

Celebrity in these terms – shallow, pseudo, fabricated, not necessarily acquainted with reality – is antithetical to the common conception of authenticity. Even on a deeper reading, the two don't fit together: authenticity has historically meant transcending society's rules, and celebrity culture is a reflection of them. You could easily argue that celebrities are inauthentic by definition. Yet without authenticity-intrigue, celebrity culture could not exist. The whole sparkling charade is only interesting because of what's going on backstage – what has evolved, since Debord and Boorstin, from gossip and scandal to confessional interviews and paparazzi, and then to pregnancy reveals and typo-ridden Instagram captions. The ordinary humanness of it all is, and always has been, what props up the glamour and the artifice.

When social media exploded in the early 2010s, the public no longer relied on journalists and paparazzi to document the lives of the actors and singers they worshipped. Celebrities suddenly had the power to expose themselves. In the past decade celebrities have attempted the impossible: to be authentic.

Yet while social media created an opportunity to prove your authenticity like never before, it also enabled people to hide who they were behind their online image – which itself led to a more fervent societal anxiety about the authenticity of others. And so as the meaning and significance of authenticity spiralled, we still clung to it as a central thread. Celebrity culture was a means by which to test our new tool. Could social media confirm that stars really were just like us? More importantly – as authentic tropes became performative, social media made celebrities of ordinary people and the boundaries of the spectacle collapsed in on themselves – could it confirm that stars really were just like themselves?

*

Like almost every term repeated endlessly on the internet, 'relatability' – a clumsy derivative of 'to relate', used for the first time in the 1960s[5] – has been condensed into cliché. Literally, being relatable could refer to any kind of connection or identification with another person but, in practice, it is overwhelmingly used to describe a generic self-sabotaging personality that leans towards extremes. It is relatable to lie in bed all day; it is also relatable to try to cram too much into the day. It is relatable to run out of money; it is relatable to want more money; it is relatable to spend a lot of money on something frivolous but not on something sensible. It is relatable to have a panic attack. It is relatable to eat burgers; it is relatable to forget to eat; it is relatable to eat salad and not enjoy it; it is relatable to eat in bed. It is not relatable to resist sleeping with your ex, and it is not relatable to have a gym membership. It is not relatable to attend the party of a close friend in good faith or to get an early night because you are tired (this changes if you are also depressed). It is not relatable to get married. Relatability, in short, suggests mess.

You can tell someone else is relatable because you are the one doing the relating. Authenticity, by contrast, is more difficult to define in objective terms. To be authentic is to realise some inner truth in the world, so while your own authenticity manifests as a feeling, someone else's is necessarily limited to appearance. This means – putting aside the obvious paradox that authenticity can only be expressed via performance – that it relies on symbolism to be tangible. That's where relatability comes in. Relatability is meaningful, as per the online cliché, when it is represented by behaviour that would typically be embarrassing, by traits that would ordinarily be kept hidden. There is, then, significant overlap between the relatable and the authentic – but only by coincidence.

The fascination with famous people doing ordinary things began in earnest in the early 2000s, when Hollywood socialites like Paris Hilton and Kim Kardashian were, to use the now more common version of Boorstin's phrase, 'famous for being famous', knocking around Beverly Hills falling out of taxis and covering their hangovers with bug-eye glasses. They were shameless in their self-promotion, armed with publicists and strategists to make a press event out of their every move. Their behaviour wasn't exactly ordinary, but it was objectively uninteresting; what their publicists knew was that it was made interesting purely by its capture on camera. And where before paparazzi had been concerned with catching the extraordinary on camera, now they weren't so fussed: *Us Weekly*'s 'Stars – They're Just Like Us' feature, which originated in an editorial meeting in 2002 when a shot of Drew Barrymore picking up a penny in the street had landed on the desk,[6] propelled a fascination with celebrities and the mundane. The column religiously ran unflattering photos of celebrities eating fast food, going to the dry cleaners, wearing tracksuits, and on and on.

In the celebrity world, being extraordinary is the norm. It follows, then, that what is ordinary elsewhere is here not only 'relatable' but subversive. On *The Simple Life*,[7] in the early 2000s, Hilton and her friend Nicole Richie made a point out of how out of touch they were by attempting to do normal jobs with disastrous consequences, making it clear that any picture of their mundanity painted by the press was still transgressive, that their fame in itself was still something worth watching. Two decades later, we have an online habit of declaring celebrities 'iconic', which is deliberately extended to examples of them doing relatable, or even embarrassing, things (Hilton and Richie, incidentally, often take on a particularly nostalgic type of iconicness). This could be read as ironic, but on a closer reading we can see it's sincere. When Beyoncé gave birth to twins in 2017, she posted a photo shoot on Instagram[8] in which she was cast as the Madonna in a Botticelli painting – a genuinely iconic image if there ever was one. But our overexposure to this type of image diminishes their power to induce revery. What was traditionally iconic has become commonplace, while sneak peeks of celebrities' real, unstaged lives are worthy of worship.

During the 2010s our appetite for celebrity authenticity was insatiable. Social media created greater scope for lies but also much greater scope for truth – and, it turned out, we preferred truth. It flattened celebrities and the public, previously two distinct factions of society, into one tweeting, posting mass. *Us Weekly* had been saying stars were 'Just Like Us' since 2002, and now the stars could prove it. The more they shared the inanities of their real lives in pictures where we knew they were holding the camera, the more we gawped at the new spectacle. And as soon as it became clear that it was a spectacle – one in which they could deliberately make themselves appear more ordinary, more present – things became complicated.

*

Even if it remains believable, an excess of relatability can be a problem for celebrities. They are supposed to be our heroes. If they are really, genuinely just like us, the system collapses. We allow them their riches and privileges, pay them our money and talk about them with our friends because we feel, on some level, they deserve it. We lay sycophantic sacrifices at online shrines so that they give back morsels of their wisdom and evidence of their superior way of living for us to aspire to. If celebrities are not special – if they are a little too much like the rest of us – there can be no such relationship.

Relatability manifests in performance, which needs an audience – a relatee, perhaps, for every relator. This process of relating, of watching celebrities be celebrities and working out which elements of their lives we understood, played out on a manic loop in the 2010s as social media culture as we know it developed and a new level of exposure became possible. But after reaching a peak in the middle of the decade relatability grew increasingly laboured and less desirable. It was tiresomely repetitious – and its performance undermined the authenticity it was supposed to signify. When Jennifer

Lawrence tripped on her gown on the stairs to the stage when she collected her Oscar in 2013, it was endearing. When she fell again on the red carpet at the Oscars in 2014, at the premiere of X-Men: Days of Future Past two months later, and then again at the X-Men: Apocalypse premiere in 2016, it became suspicious (questions about whether the fall had been faked abounded online). Relatability was once an exposure, authored in some way by Lawrence herself, but it soon became the facade. What was she hiding underneath the girl-next-door shtick?

Lawrence, a statuesque beauty who was for two years the highest-paid actress in the world, clearly leaned into her relatable attributes that satisfied the public desire for authenticity at the same time her success peaked. It wasn't her fault that celebrity culture and the press amplified it to its extreme and created an exponential curve of exposure that ultimately looped back on itself. She and her relatable love of fast food were everywhere. The press pitted her affectionately against the rest of the fake Hollywood world as cutely flawed and down-to-earth with endless, almost impressively inane headlines. 'Juliane Moore on Jennifer Lawrence: "She's a Genuinely Authentic Individual"'.[9] 'Jennifer Lawrence's Singing Voice is Awesomely Awful'.[10] 'Just When You Think Jennifer Lawrence Can't Fit Another Marshmallow In Her Mouth, She Surprises You'.[11] For almost all of 2013, Vulture ran a regular feature called 'This Week in Jennifer Lawrence Quotes'. The online headline for her Vogue cover story in 2015, a year in which she had earned $52m at the age of 25,[12] read: 'Jennifer Lawrence Is Determined, Hilarious, and – Above

All – *Real*'.[13] For those who, relatably, couldn't be bothered to read the piece, the *Hollywood Reporter* ran a helpful follow-up: 'The 5 Most Relatable Moments from Jennifer Lawrence's *Vogue* Interview'.[14]

Sycophancy soon slid into derision. Ariana Grande imitated her unfavourably on *Saturday Night Live* in 2016 ('They told me not to do a game show,' she said, affecting a husky register, 'but I was like, screw it, I can have fun, I'm a regular person').[15] Lawrence's relatability – with all the protection it had offered her in a media landscape that remained at its heart cruel, misogynistic and reactionary – was defunct. It had become clear that authenticity and relatability were not synonymous – and that authenticity was still paramount. Confessing something embarrassing was exposed as just an easy, obvious way of revealing what's underneath the surface while still conforming to expectations. And pretending to be authentic was almost worse than not being authentic in the first place.

Authenticity demands that we *don't* conform to expectations: that we are purely, exquisitely ourselves; that our inner self overcomes any constraints the outer world may impose. In 2015 another headline in *Elle* read: 'An Ode To Jennifer Lawrence Being Her Most Jennifer Lawrence Self On The 'Hunger Games' Red Carpet'.[16] We didn't just want celebrities to be like us – we wanted them to be themselves.

★

17

Celebrities provide an aspirational model for how to live; their lifestyles are 'an articulation of basic American/Western values',[17] wrote Dyer. Now, when arguably the most basic Western value is that we should all find our true selves and live according to them, we idolise those we perceive to be living in line with their authentic truth. Jennifer Lawrence ultimately gave the sense that she was playing herself rather than being herself – that she was less like Jennifer Lawrence than she was pretending to be. But elsewhere in the celebrity world, it seems that if you do it right, it's impossible to be too much of yourself. For example, Kim Kardashian is plainly more like Kim Kardashian than Kim Kardashian actually is. She has even made herself look more like herself through gradual and subtle tweaks – her small nose appears slightly smaller, her full lips slightly fuller, her curves slightly curvier. Yet, unlike Lawrence, who is famous for the traditional reason of being an actress, Kim Kardashian is Kim Kardashian precisely because she is Kim Kardashian, and so the more like Kim Kardashian she can be, the better. Or, to put it another way: the more a Noughties socialite dilutes herself into a super-concentrated sellable essence, the richer she gets.

Kardashian is the ultimate example of Boorstin's human pseudo-event. She has only ever been known for her well-knownness. In the early 2000s she made her name by deliberately drawing attention to herself on the Hollywood social scene alongside Hilton and Richie. Everything about them was controlled and owned. During these years, a strong sense of individual identity – what we would later call a 'personal brand' – became, for celebrities, not a means to an end but an end in itself.

Kardashian has now pushed the personal brand to its final form. In 2007, a few months after her sex tape had been leaked online (it was reportedly bought for $1m by Vivid Entertainment in what Ray J – the other party in the video – told the *Daily Mail* was set up as a planned deal),[18] her new reality show aired. *Keeping Up With The Kardashians*[19] followed Kim, her mother and her sisters (the family of OJ Simpson's lawyer and close friend Robert Kardashian, who died in 2003) in their day-to-day lives. Three years after it began, Instagram launched. Twitter already had 54 million users. Social media made it even easier for the Kardashians to achieve what they were attempting to with *Keeping Up*: the sweet spot of glamour and candour that has always been the foundation for celebrity culture. The Kardashians were their own paparazzi, appearing to share so much that there was nothing left for a scoop, yet still managing to make headlines with the trivialities that occurred on the show and on their feeds. As the show trundled along, Kim nurtured her personal brand online, giving her followers yet more access to the self she was already baring on the TV. The only difference between her and a 'real' celebrity was that every element of her fame was deliberate. This cynicism built into the Kardashian brand has long functioned as an excuse for their capturing so much attention. There is an honesty to their fakeness, and therefore an 'authenticity' to how they actually live, that has enabled their fame.

The celebrity spectacle has become a performance of truth-living. Prince Harry and Meghan Markle's choice to cut themselves off from the royal family in 2020 was ostensibly a response to the attacks on Markle by the British media[20] but was narrativised equally as a move towards authenticity and a rejection of the structures imposed on them. In the interview that followed with Oprah Winfrey in March 2021,[21] Harry said that his relatives were 'trapped within the system', and Markle said she and Harry were 'able to live more authentically' in their California mansion; filmed outside on the sunny patio, they appeared to be the easy-going, 'real' antidote to the stuffiness and traditionalism of the institution. They were now equipped to be celebrities proper because they were leaning in not to any established system but individual truth-living. That might look different from the Kardashians' truths, but the process is the same.

The Oprah interview was significant in what it revealed – the main headline was the alleged concern of a royal family member over how dark-skinned Harry and Meghan's baby might be[22] – but also in that it happened in the first place. In modern celebrity, the way you choose to tell your story is as significant as the story itself (not telling it at all would undermine your celebrity status as somebody worthy of watching). Harry and Meghan were predictably criticised for giving the interview: Piers Morgan called them 'hypocritical, professional victims'[23] for leaving the UK to escape the public eye and then immediately going back into it; their mistake, if they made one at all, was not in speaking but in ever attempting privacy. 'If there's something that we're going through, it's going to get out anyway,' Kim Kardashian told *Glamour* magazine in 2011, discussing *Keeping Up With The Kardashians*. 'It'll be on the cover of a tabloid, and it'll be twisted the completely wrong way. So why not tell our story?'[24]

A commitment to self-authorship means that any fakeness can simply be subsumed into the overall narrative: the very admission of it connotes authenticity. The Kardashians, in a sense, live a triple life – one on the show, one on social media and one in reality. That we might only be able to access one of those lives at once – notwithstanding our right to scroll our phones at the same time as watching TV – leaves us wanting more; that we know all the layers are out there somewhere contributes to the feeling of transparency. Kim Kardashian committed to exposure by growing her social media following and ensuring her tendency to post and share was not just a means to communicate her personal brand but a part of what she was communicating. She performed her own performance, cameras capturing cameras. 'Kim,' her mother, Kris Jenner, says in one famous scene in *Keeping Up With The Kardashians* as Kim preens with a digital camera in a moving car, 'would you stop taking pictures of yourself? Your sister's going to jail.'[25]

In this world, authenticity is not sold as a question of real or fake, truth or lie – it wouldn't be viable because it is lies and fakery all the way through. It is sold as a confession, as owning up to one's fakeness. The Kardashians have never pretended to be anything other than what they are, which is manufactured and materialistic. As long as they admitted any fakery, they were bulletproof. In an episode of *Keeping Up*

21

With The Kardashians in 2015,[26] the older sisters coach Kylie Jenner, the youngest (from Kris Jenner's second marriage), on the importance of doing this. Kylie, then aged 17, had recently drastically changed the appearance of her lips, quite obviously with injectable filler, and marketed the transformation by creating and heavily promoting a makeup 'lip kit'. Reporters were beginning to ask questions about what she'd done. The episode's main plot line is Kylie coming to terms with how she should, in the words of her older sister Khloé, 'cop up to' the procedure (early in the episode, we watch Khloé candidly having cellulite lasered off her buttocks). She begins by saying that she's 'never' going to 'confirm or deny anything' about her lips. (That statement is itself extraordinary given she is being filmed for a show, on which she is one of the main characters, that has already revealed in plain terms that her lips have been filled.) In the end, with the encouragement of Kim and Khloé, she is reformed. 'If my sisters can own up to their insecurities, so can I,' she says. This framing of the surgery as an admission of insecurity, as some external manifestation of an inner truth, renders it authentic. Jenner was praised as brave and honest, and her lips are still the most famous thing about her.

Similarly, the Kardashians' lack of grace surrounding their wealth appears to be the opposite of the relatable, down-to-earth celebrity model but, in fact, plays into their authenticity. Just like their allegiance to their perfectly constructed selves, earning enormous amounts of money is presented unabashedly as a worthwhile goal that's part of the brand. In March 2019 Kylie was declared by *Forbes* to be the world's youngest 'self-made' billionaire at the age of 21.[27] That this turned out not to be true – it was calculated using dodgy figures that *Forbes* later revealed in a slightly resentful article clarifying that in fact Jenner was only worth a diminutive $900m[28] – did not prevent it from contributing to Jenner's perceived 'authenticity'. The 'self-made' narrative helps to sell the idea that they are not only famous for being famous, or even famous simply for being themselves, but famous – and rich – for their unique ability to make themselves more famous and rich. When Kim herself was put on the cover of *Forbes* in 2016 with the tagline 'How anyone with a following can cash in',[29] she tweeted, knowingly: 'Not bad for a girl with no talent'.[30] In a convoluted way, this is peak authenticity: performing winking self-awareness to your millions of followers to flaunt your very real money.

The urge to position celebrities as grafters in this way is a testament to authenticity's continued reign over celebrity culture. It offsets any suggestion that you could be there through luck, balances the ordinary (work) with the extraordinary (success), and also implies that you have worked to realise the inner truth of who you are (that is, the successful person you now present to the world). In 2022 the influencer Molly-Mae Hague was widely criticised for commenting as a podcast guest on Steven Bartlett's *Diary of a CEO* that 'everyone has the same twenty-four hours in a day',[31] largely because the twenty-four hours of the garment workers for PrettyLittleThing, the fast-fashion company for which she is creative director, undoubtedly feel substantially different from hers. Though the criticisms of Hague were worthwhile, it is unfortunate for her that there was such an obvious point of comparison, since the sentiment underlines the entirety of influencer culture: anyone can be a celebrity by commodifying their selfhood, and doing so somehow constitutes worthwhile work. In an interview with *Variety* in early 2022, Kardashian's advice to women in business was to 'get your fucking ass up and work. It seems like nobody wants to work these days.'[32] No talent, just work: what could be more authentic than that?

*

When Kim Kardashian entered into a public row with Taylor Swift in 2017, supposedly in defence of her husband, Kanye West, it was clear that the celebrity world had split in two. The argument concerned West referring to Swift in his song 'Famous' as 'that bitch'[33] – a line she said she hadn't consented to and found misogynistic, and which followed a previous feud. Kardashian said Swift was lying, and that she had a recording of the phone conversation when Swift gave West the go-ahead. Kardashian posted that recording – in which Swift did not appear explicitly to approve the wording 'that bitch' but did discuss other elements of the song with West – to her Snapchat. Kardashian framed Swift's outrage at the song as a publicity grab at the expense of West.

Swift was being accused of something slightly different from inauthenticity. In fact, given Swift has always retained careful control over her public image, she upheld her personal brand immaculately. During the row with Kardashian, she communicated using carefully worded statements from her team (while Kardashian posted on Snapchat with a decade of self-baring as a foundation). Instead, Swift was implicitly accused, first by Kardashian and then by the online mob, of insincerity: misrepresenting herself in a way that somehow bent the social structure out of shape. Both concepts are concerned with realising 'who I am' but differ in their definition of 'who' and 'I', as well as the ultimate purpose of being true to it: 'If one is true to one's own self for the purpose of avoiding falsehood to others,' Lionel Trilling asks in *Sincerity and Authenticity*, 'is one being truly true to one's own self?'[34]

The Kardashian–Swift row was, as Anna Leszkiewicz wrote in the *New Statesman* at the time, 'a battle between two very different types of storytelling',[35] with the question of 'avoiding falsehood to others' at its heart. Unlike Kardashian's honest fakeness, Swift's public image was one of cultivated authenticity. She was unashamedly goofy and wholesome, her saccharine pop infused with country and acoustic guitar, her Instagram feed carefully populated with photos of cats and playful screenshots of her messages with Ed Sheeran. She was, in a way, relatable. She was not playing a celebrity like the Kardashians and only playing herself to a certain extent – a textbook example of a star who was just like us but clearly better: more successful, more beautiful, more talented. The characters Swift adopts in her songs are often exaggerated to create a dramatic and more immediately relatable narrative, which constitutes a huge part of their listening appeal. But Kardashian said Swift had always done well out of 'playing the victim'.[36]

Celebrity alter egos and personas can actively contribute to their perception as authentic, but only when the process of adopting it is also an exercise in truth-living. Lady Gaga once described herself as 'a show with no intermission';[37] in a profile of her for the *New York Times Magazine* in 2018, Rachel Syme wrote that 'instead of seeing those identities as segmented – the real person, the facade – she put forth the concept that it's possible... to try to free yourself from old boundaries'.[38] David Bowie (whom Gaga idolises)[39] shape-shifted for his whole career, and each persona was expressed in his music. Beyoncé said that her alter ego, Sasha Fierce, 'protects me and who I really am'.[40] After the row between Swift and Kardashian, during which armies of fans had been unleashed online by each side and Kardashian's spill-all methods had come out on top, Swift re-emerged the following year in a new mean-girl character. She released a musically hollow revenge track, 'Look What You Made Me Do',[41] as the lead single for her new album, *Reputation*. In the video, she draped herself in snakes in reference to a pointed tweet by Kardashian involving an enthusiastic use of the snake emoji. To hammer home the point, Swift (who has always had an eye for drama) deleted every previous post on her Instagram. But Swift's revenge persona appeared inauthentic, which is to say not in alignment with her inner truth, because she had previously projected an image of someone who did not need a persona in the first place. Any inauthenticity was less about the actual character – the consensus was that Swift probably was genuinely gunning for revenge – and more about the creation of it. It was not sufficiently protective of her real self to represent freedom.

*

If social media makes the unreal seem real, reality TV does the reverse. *An American Family,*[42] broadcast in the US in 1973 and often referenced as the first true reality TV show, followed a middle-class white family in California through their daily lives, which ultimately included the parents' divorce. It was not, as sister Khloé once described *Keeping Up With The Kardashians* (and unlike contemporary iterations such as *Love Island*), the equivalent of a 'thirty-minute commercial',[43] nor did it involve anyone who was already in the limelight. It was a supposedly honest depiction of ordinary life. Yet for all its mundane intentions, the family in question, the Louds, later complained that the material had been edited to emphasise the negative elements of their dynamic. Critics at the time were sceptical of the extent to which the footage could be 'real' in the first place because the presence of a camera naturally encourages performance.

In reality TV, the creation of drama and narrative by the presence of the camera is not incidental. It is deliberate, just as it was for Paris Hilton. In a 2011 piece for the *New York Times* on *Cinema Verite*, the HBO film about the making of *An American Family*, Dennis Lim noted 'the potential function of the camera as a catalyst, not simply an observer'.[44] The camera-as-catalyst underlies the whole genre: the camera 'catalyses' or amplifies the behaviours and expressions of the individuals involved, just as early critics worried it would; it is also a symbol of the show's existence. It is all that is necessary to bring someone else's 'reality' to our screen. It catalyses, even crystallises, not only what happens within the show but the genre's fundamental process – the turning of real situations into unreal ones.

Reality TV represents a circular type of authenticity. Its unique purpose is to be 'real', of course, and yet the primary criticism of it is usually that it is fake (we now know, for example, from reports of prior contestants, that seemingly spontaneous or genuine conversations have in fact been engineered by producers, filmed over and over again until they serve their narrative purpose). The rapid evolution of the genre after *An American Family* – when production houses realised that it was much cheaper and equally entertaining to lock fifteen extroverts in a house together than to hire a scriptwriter – also meant that reality TV was a one-way ticket to celebrity, a social status with a confused relationship with authenticity. Reality TV celebrity only further clouds the relationship: this type of fame, explicitly engineered, involves play-acting at being a celebrity while you and your followers know you are actually a normal person.

In other words, reality TV also turns real people into unreal ones. It takes the authenticity that society hankers after and manipulates it until it resembles the confused version that manifests in celebrity culture; or, put more simply, it takes humans and turns them into pseudo-events (where once the goal for a *Big Brother* housemate might have been to be a TV presenter, now a stint on a reality TV show provides a path towards an influencing career). On now-defunct talent shows like *The X Factor,* this transformation played out crudely. Contestants who made it far enough were given a makeover and the opportunity to perform like a real pop star with dancers and light shows and a screaming crowd, and then swiftly pushed down the chute back to reality when they were voted off (former contestants have since complained about the lack of 'aftercare'). Even those who successfully transition from a show contestant to a 'celebrity' usually appear qualitatively different from Hollywood actors and pop stars. Reality TV transports people living real lives into a world of performance, but it also undermines any of the inherent reality of that new world. This kind of celebrity is paper-thin, both too much like us and made to appear miles away.

In 'scripted reality' shows such as *The Only Way is Essex* and *Made in Chelsea,* the question of authenticity is even less clear. But the mass appeal of this type of show, in which real people are inserted into real situations – restaurants and bars, rather than a mansion with a diary room – for the sole reason that a producer has told them to, is that they create more, even endless, 'reality'. By engineering drama, in the same way a soap opera script would, structured reality forces real human reactions and relationships, fulfilling the urge for authenticity despite being fake. Similarly, traditional reality shows, from *Big Brother* to cookery competitions, often regenerate with a 'celebrity' version. This is a direct reversal of the initial trajectory of ordinary to extraordinary: it places the celebrity – who is often in need of a career boost – back into reality[45] (or some bizarre version of it).

29

Reality TV shows that involve audience participation tend to reflect directly the processes that underlie celebrity culture. They are crude demonstrations of democratised celebrity.[46] We, the audience, watch a show – say, *Love Island* – and keep the people we like on our screens by voting for them. Generally, the longer someone lasts on *Love Island*, the more famous they'll be at the end, and the better equipped they'll be to set up a swimwear range or tooth-whitening kit to sell on Instagram. Once that has happened, we vote for them over and over again by following them, liking their posts and, possibly, buying said swimwear or tooth-whitening kit. There is very little of the mystique that is appealing in real celebrities (somehow, it's difficult to imagine Rihanna walking into a meeting in which her publicist offers her the opportunity to model some bikinis or get paid to drink a protein shake) but it is reassuring, in a way, to know that these particular stars really are just like us.

When we are asked to vote for *Love Island* contestants, the criteria are very different from those of, say, *X Factor* contestants. Talent shows have faded into insignificance; budding pop stars are more likely to find their own audience online. On *Love Island* – which is based on the *Big Brother* model but with the bonus of contestants needing to be young, single and attractive in order to participate – there is, per Kim Kardashian, no need to demonstrate any particular talent. Broadly, you must simply excel at being yourself. Some contestants, such as 2018's Dani Dyer, are lauded for their apparent genuineness; some, such as 2019's Maura Higgins, are adored for their straight-talking extroversion and their ability to perform their own personality. They are celebrated for being themselves, for living their truth. This is authenticity for authenticity's sake.

Reality TV is no longer concerned with simply depicting unfiltered reality – I've got enough reality on my phone, thanks. Instead, it stays relevant by advocating for living your truth at all costs. Where traditional celebrities have failed to provide adequate examples for us to emulate in the art of being yourself – too fake, too talented, too rich – reality stars were, not so long ago, completely ordinary and, as it happens, are exquisitely, expertly themselves. No matter how shallow or immoral their pursuits – take *Love Island* prodigy Molly-Mae Hague's fast-fashion career – they are protected by the armour of authenticity. Extracting ourselves from this web of performance for a moment, we might remember that 'living your truth' is, in epistemological terms, a nonsensical statement: everything you do is 'truth' in that it is happening in objective reality. And so, in the world of reality TV, which includes the online world that follows it, fakery and immorality become authentic, just like they do for the Kardashians. Plastic surgery and heavily edited photographs are living out the truth of your insecurities. Choosing to participate in the artifice of reality TV is authentically trying to reach your full potential as an influencer. Partnering with an exploitative fashion brand is truthfully realising your capabilities as a model. Truth-living trumps everything, and so all action is afforded equal weight.

Similarly, the construction of a persona is the ultimate tribute to the art of celebrity. Reality TV culture has come full circle in this sense: it deliberately creates fakeness in order to emulate a celebrity culture in which people have historically tried desperately to convey authenticity. Perhaps this is because authenticity has never really been in question for people who have lived with cameras in their shower; to elevate themselves to the height of a public figure, they have to balance this ordinariness, this presence, with a little bit of extraordinariness and absence. Gemma Collins, who became famous through *The Only Way is Essex* and has continued to build her brand on *Celebrity Big Brother, I'm A Celebrity... Get Me Out of Here!, Celebs Go Dating, Dancing On Ice, Celebrity MasterChef* and her own reality series, *Gemma Collins: Diva Forever,* is notably straight-talking and relatable. She is also known, a decade into her career, for her persona. While Gemma Collins is the person who 'still [puts her] own washing in',[47] The GC is glamorous, Collins's famous 'diva'. 'The GC is a character, and she's hilarious,' Collins told *Vice.*[48]

Collins's flaunting of The GC as a separate entity might seem to contradict the notion that celebrities should simply be themselves, but it is an extension of the same idea. Collins, like Kim Kardashian, found the loophole. It doesn't matter how many layers of persona you have, so long as all of them are public. Collins reveals her 'real self' on social media and in interviews; The GC is deployed on TV. It is with maximum authenticity in mind that this is confessed as well as simply enacted. As well as a type of sincerity – making sure her position in society as a big-C celebrity is absolutely clear – this signifies what the crowd wants to hear: that Gemma Collins knows herself. The acknowledgement of both layers reveals in the crudest possible terms that she has an inner self and that she is giving us the privilege of seeing it. The persona, far from hiding the truth, actively contributes to her perceived authenticity.

*

Since the mid-2010s Jennifer Lawrence fever and the celebrity world's frantic push for authenticity, public desires have shifted somewhat. There is a sense of social media over-saturation and an increasing consensus that we would no longer like to watch stars doing ordinary things – rather, we would like them to put on a show again. Yet this doesn't mean we are any less in the grip of authenticity: in fact, it means we would like stars – for all their natural extraordinariness – to be more themselves than ever.

Boorstin drew a distinction between celebrities and heroes, which we might interpret to be inauthentic and authentic idols, but there is no longer a simple dichotomy. He wrote, strikingly: 'We can make a celebrity, but we can never make a hero. In a now-almost-forgotten sense, all heroes are self-made.'[49] The Kardashians are, on this reading, both celebrities and heroes, both fake and real. He continued: 'The hero was distinguished by his achievement; the celebrity by his image or trademark. The hero created himself; the celebrity is created by the media. The hero was a big man; the celebrity is a big name.'[50]

Across celebrity culture, we see that this is no longer the case. Celebrities have come full circle in their attempts to be authentic, but they cannot be categorised as wholly inauthentic, either. Like Boorstin's hero, the celebrity must be a 'big man' to survive – that is, have a powerful sense of individual self, displayed for all to see. The celebrity no longer relies on the media: he creates himself by posting on social media. The celebrity is defined by his image – but it must be one of his true self. And finding this self, and then living its truth in public, is all you need to achieve to become a star.

ART

In her essay *Exposure*,[1] the novelist Olivia Sudjic observes that 'while writing can contribute to a feeling of unreality (going mad), reading others' outpourings usually has the opposite effect'.[2] She reads, she suggests, to 'feel alive from a safe distance'.[3] In an essay about the sensation of being perceived as an artist and the question of self within a work, this idea stands out. Sudjic writes of how women's work is dissected and analysed as 'autofiction'; when women write fiction it is read as truth, she says, and when they write truth it is read as lies.[4] She exposes – through a feminist lens – that we are obsessed with art being authentic. And yet if writing makes us unreal, and reading does the opposite, we understand that art's 'authenticity' is not so much about the genuineness of the author as the feelings it evokes in the reader.

It is perhaps our desire to see ourselves reflected in someone else, in order to better know who we are, that has fuelled the contemporary fixation on the genre of autofiction – that is, a novel based on the author's life. If the author makes themselves vulnerable by baring their inner self in this way, the reader can be buoyed and reassured in their own authenticity – or they can be made fluid by their immersion in the world of such a strong 'other'. When the author's identity is established and certain, the reader has the opportunity to become unfixed, feeling sufficiently anchored by the author that their thoughts and self-perception can wander freely. This can manifest as a certain kind of relatability, where we are able to understand ourselves better in light of someone else's self-revelations – or we might feel that the work captures and expresses our own feelings or experience better than we ever could. Whatever art offers when it exposes in some way the inner life of another person, immersing yourself fully in it requires submission. It's a trust exercise.

Susan Choi's 2019 novel of that name, set in a theatre school in an unnamed US city, interrogates the boundaries of autobiographical fiction and the role of authenticity within it. We learn that acting is 'fidelity to authentic emotion, under imagined circumstances':[5] *Trust Exercise* is a novel that invites us to question whether we can rely on its narrators to tell the truth while also interrogating the limits of fiction itself – the role of reality in unreality and vice versa. It opens as a coming-of-age love story, written from Sarah's perspective in the third person. She is embroiled in an intense romance with another student, David. Their teacher, Mr Kingsley, pushes her to own up to her authentic emotions in a series of humiliating trust exercises in front of the class. She goes to parties, sleeps with men, and walks for hours to get home. However, just as the story of this clammy teen world reaches a climax, it is interrupted. The narrative is switched to a new section, entitled: 'Trust Exercise'.

There is a different narrator now: 'Karen' – a name we've heard before. '"Karen" is not "Karen's" name, but "Karen" knew, when she read her name "Karen," that it was she who was meant,' Karen writes.[6] She has discovered that her old friend Sarah has written a book about their time at theatre school and that she has been sidelined, her truth concealed. Karen proceeds to fill in the gaps, switching between the first and third person, burning with rage both at what happened to her and her insignificance in Sarah's story. 'Like Chekhov says. "If we're going to hear a gun in Act Two, we've got to see it in Act One"', Karen explains during rehearsals for a play in the novel's second section. 'Actually, he says that if we see it in Act One, it's got to go off by Act Two,' she is corrected. 'But, same difference.'[7]

In *Trust Exercise* Choi exposes that fiction cannot encompass everyone's truth at once. As we become increasingly gripped by the idea that we must all be authentic, we search across the artistic spectrum (in fiction but also, notably, in pop music) for traces of self that could be translated onto our own selves in turn – a phenomenon that has led to unwelcome probes into artists' work, debates about who gets to tell certain stories, and, in some cases, new ways of making art.

*

Referring specifically to autofiction, a genre that throws the collision of the real and the imagined into stark light, Brigitte Weingart, a media theorist at Berlin's University of the Arts, wrote in 2019 that 'if our so-called life events are traded as a valuable resource, especially on social media, this has to have an impact on literary production'.[8] In the publishing market, the increasing dominance of books that are sold as 'raw' and relatable reflects the public desire for selfhood to be narrativised – as does the fervent discussion, across journalism and publishing, of the autofiction trend. The term was first used by Serge Doubrovsky in 1977 to describe his novel *Fils*, but is now applied broadly to apparently any fictional work with autobiographical elements. By today's standards, the label 'autofiction' could retrospectively be applied to countless novels published before interrogation of the boundary between the real and imagined became so routine (take D. H. Lawrence's *Sons and Lovers*,[9] or Charles Dickens's *David Copperfield,* for example). The contemporary fascination with the genre is powered by our obsession with authenticity. The focus of conversations about autofiction is on selfhood and its legitimacy, both in the internal narrative of the works themselves and the broader, evolving, literary canon. Labelling a work as 'autofiction' points out what was previously implicit – that a work combines the real and the imagined – and its application can curdle the mixture.

When Karen reviews Sarah's autobiographical novel in *Trust Exercise*, she sneers that 'the scheme is almost too simple – out of respect for the "truth"? From a failure of imagination? Is it better or worse that the code is so easy to crack?'[10] Worse, surely: autofiction's 'authenticity' is its fatal flaw. It may be true to its creator, but in doing so it is disarmingly untrue to its medium – it is inauthentic in its status as *fiction*. If something that passes for a novel is, in fact, partly a memoir, how do we know what we're getting? As a reader, there is a sense of betrayal in discovering that something presumed to be fictional is in fact based on real life. Is it not the job of the writer to innovate, to move past what's right in front of them? And if writing a novel is simply a question of telling your own story, something we all have, could we not all do it? The sudden, overt presence of autobiography can puncture the solitary, intimate experience of reading fiction, leaving us disillusioned: I came here for an escape, and all I got was this lousy reality.

It is clear that the tangible presence of the author in a work doesn't necessarily lead to an authentic experience for the reader: in fact, the opposite can be true. Early twentieth century modernist literature, as Lionel Trilling writes, is 'shockingly personal – it asks us if we are content with our marriages, with our professional lives, with our friends… It asks us if we are content with ourselves'.[11] And yet these writers were self-professedly artists over selves. James Joyce said that 'The personality of the artist… finally refines itself out of existence';[12] T. S. Eliot that 'The progress of an artist is… a continual extinction of personality'.[13] Trilling's point is that this doesn't make their work any less able to ask questions of our own authentic selves. Their truth is simply further embedded into the page.

Regardless of intention, writers have, of course, written about themselves consistently for centuries. Goethe wrote *The Sorrows of Young Werther* to process the end of a love affair. Philip Roth told the *Paris Review* in 1984 that he was 'making fake biography, false history, concocting a half-imaginary existence out of the actual drama of my life'.[14] Franz Kafka wrote that 'writing means revealing oneself to excess'.[15] More to the point, novelists have also protested at their work being reduced to such a crude binary. Nabokov was scathing in his 1944 biography of Nikolai Gogol about 'the morbid inclination we have to derive satisfaction from the fact (generally false and always irrelevant) that a work of art is traceable to a "true story"'[16] (a decade later he would publish *Lolita*, from whose narrator anyone would want to maintain significant artistic distance).

More recently, writers have (perhaps unsurprisingly) rejected the specific label of autofiction, too. As Sudjic explores in *Exposure*, the tendency to categorise women's writing as 'personal' and to fret over its authenticity more than men's – notwithstanding the quotations above – means that autofiction also now has a political connotation, which provides only more reason to question any initial misgivings about the genre we may have as readers. In 2017, around the time that her novel *I Love Dick* was experiencing a resurgence, Chris Kraus was interviewed by *The Cut*. 'All through the literature it's all autobiographical,' she said. 'It's all this male "I" talking about shit. But as soon as it's a woman talking about shit, she's only talking about herself and her problems... [The term "autofiction" is] applied to my work, and to a lot of other people's work, but I would never use it.'[17] Similarly, Jenny Offill, whose protagonists sometimes bear striking resemblances to her, has noted that focusing on the 'personal' in women's work undermines its inherent intellectual or artistic value.[18]

Women writers, in particular, are in a quandary: as much as they are undermined for creating something overtly personal, they are also expected to be authentic. As it does for anyone in the public eye, exposing vulnerability proves you are in touch with yourself – and also makes you 'relatable', allowing readers to experience their own authentic self via yours. It is not just in literary fiction that self-expurgation is encouraged and scorned in equal measure: the online 'personal essay' has boomed in a new media landscape of young editors trying to find viral hits. The divulgence of something unique and personal is, it seems, more likely to yield clicks than expert insight on a news item. Reading someone's life story is an attractive prospect mainly because you can compare it to your own and either indulge in a little *schadenfreude* or be relieved by the knowledge that you're not alone. In recent years there has been an influx of memoirs published by women under thirty, prompting questions from older people about how much life they really have to write about, but proving addictive reading material for people who are of exactly the same age and background as the author. In the early days of the novel, a patriarchal fascination with – or fear of – women's supposed mystique entrenched worries that reading would corrupt women lest they empathise too strongly with the flawed and impure characters within the

41

books and were consequently torn away from their sense of duty.[19] The modern desire for total transparency from women writers is an extension of the same concern: women are unpredictable, not to be trusted, and so exhibiting their true selves is an opportunity for the public to examine their worthiness. And perhaps women readers want to be 'corrupted' by flawed characters more than ever, seeing themselves reflected in them – less because women are severely restrained by a sense of duty and more because we are all under cultural mandate to find out who we are.

When an author withholds, they keep all the power; when they deliberately expose themselves – not only as selves but as authors – the power dynamic is reversed. Autofiction can be disarming for readers but it can also be empowering. In *Mousse* magazine in 2020, Philipp Handahl noted that auto-fiction's strength is its ability to '[lay] bare the conditions of its own production'.[20] A selfie posted to social media reveals not just the outfit you wore that day or the expression on your face, but that you got out your phone, opened the camera and stood taking pictures of yourself until you took one that you felt sufficiently captured the image of yourself that you wanted to project. In the same way, autofiction exposes a conscious artistic process.

In her 2020 novel *Fake Accounts*,[21] Lauren Oyler explores how the construction of character affects the power dynamics between author, reader and protagonist. Her nameless narrator affects new identities out of boredom; her seemingly pathological inability to be truthful to other characters within the narrative causes us to question whether we can

42

trust her. And yet she is grounded in reality – our reality – by her resemblance to Oyler, and by the novel's constant structural self-awareness and breaking of the fourth wall. Narrative sections are loudly declared: 'Beginning', 'Middle (something happens)', 'Middle (nothing happens)'. Such self-awareness empowers Oyler in her command of the narrative, but it also makes her vulnerable to the reader's gaze. When the protagonist constructs multiple personas on a dating app, she deliberately recognises her own inauthenticity: 'even the come-ons were illusory, inspired by my virtual persona and not myself'.[22] The narrator's laissez-faire attitude to her own identity is both justified and subtly ribbed by other characters – in particular the Greek chorus of 'ex-boyfriends' – who reflect and assuage the reader's frustration in the protagonist's lack of stability. Yet all such analysis comes from her own mind (both Oyler's, and the narrator's) and so she is always both one step ahead and one step behind. 'Any declarative statement about yourself would inevitably result in having to publicly revise whatever distinction you'd made,' she writes of her boyfriend, Felix's, views on identity labels, 'admitting you had not known yourself as well as you thought you did.'[23] Like Choi, Oyler shows us that reality doesn't preclude unreality, and vice versa: that 'truth' is not always about being authentic.

*

The question of ownership of a story is fundamental to the preoccupation with selfhood within art. In 2017 the

New Yorker published a short story called 'Cat Person'[24] by a then-unknown writer, Kristen Roupenian. The story is about a young woman dating an older man, whom she both likes and finds a little pathetic. In an uncomfortable sex scene, she discovers that he actually repulses her and subsequently attempts to distance herself from him. He turns on her in a twist at the end. It went viral, becoming one of their most read articles of the year, because of its almost painful relatability – its confrontation of sticky subject matter. At the time, Roupenian was subject to the usual post-facto raking over of women's work for personal influences; readers assumed the story was based on her dating history. No matter, she got a seven-figure book deal, and 'Cat Person' faded into collective online memory.

Until, that is, July 2021, when a personal essay appeared on *Slate*: '"Cat Person" and Me' by Alexis Nowicki, for whom the seeming authenticity of 'Cat Person' took on a different meaning. 'The similarities to my own life were eerie,' she wrote. '… Could it be a wild coincidence? Or did Roupenian, a person I'd never met, somehow know about me?'[25]

In the wake of her newfound fame, Roupenian had told the *New Yorker* that the story had been inspired by a nasty experience online.[26] When the *New York Times* asked her if that was true, she replied: 'I wrote the story immediately after the encounter… It's not autobiographical; though many of the details and emotional notes come from life, they were accumulated over decades.'[27] It turned out that the 'encounter' in question was real: it took place between Nowicki and her ex-boyfriend. He had told Roupenian about his and Nowicki's relationship, which resulted, as Roupenian explained in an email to Nowicki (published in the *Slate* piece), in her '[writing] a story that was primarily a work of the imagination, but which also drew on my own personal experiences, both past and present'.[28] She then explained that she felt it was essential for her, in the wake of the story going viral and subsequent aggression from (male) readers, to separate her personal life and her fiction – to make it plain the story wasn't real. But, of course, the story became real as soon as it was read by anyone who saw themselves in it: it went viral because of some widely acknowledged 'truth' that it uncovered. It just wasn't necessarily Roupenian's story to tell.

We are drawn to these stories partly because they concern the near-universal and justifiably concerning topic of privacy. They expose how the internet, in particular, blurs the boundaries of what is ours. In 2021 an article called 'Who Is the Bad Art Friend?',[29] published in the *New York Times*, told the story of two writers: one of them liked to share intimate details of her life online – namely, her donation of a kidney – and the other took those details and put them in her work, to the first's great distress, leading ultimately to a legal dispute. Though we are not all in writers' groups or in the habit of donating kidneys, plenty of us are making ourselves characters on social media. If someone uses something we have made public for their art, can we say we still own it, given their interaction with it is equally a part of their subjective experience as the actual event is ours? Are they taking part of what is truly us, or are they taking something already made-up?

Whether or not it is justifiable in this way, the adoption of another person's experience for your own gain is bound to have an emotional impact on that person. It removes agency. The subject of the story does not have the opportunity to tell it on their own terms; Nowicki, in fact, said that 'Cat Person' made her doubt her own memory of events and wonder whether her ex was actually worse than she remembered.[30] But, as we learn from Nowicki, the 'Bad Art Friend' and from *Trust Exercise*, this of course only comes to light when the reader of the work is the person whose truth has been mangled. That readers tend to happily accept a writer's authority on a topic is partly why the question of 'authenticity' – of a writer's being true to themselves – seems so important. Authenticity here is not just about individual truth but collective truth, and therefore underlines one of the foremost debates of our time: is it acceptable to write from the point of view of a character whose life experience is drastically different from yours, or should you only write what you know?

It's easy to see how this question further propels the personal writing economy, which necessarily includes the sometimes unwelcome interest in the source material for writers' work. Writers can insulate themselves from the accusation that they have claimed someone else's truth for their own by writing about themselves; the right to recount one's own experiences is incontrovertible. The 'autofiction' label, or even the 'personal essay' rubric accompanying an online article, provide a safety net for both the reader and the writer, guaranteeing that the author will not slip up and comment inappropriately on somebody else's culture or identity – tell someone else's story.

The historic and ongoing lack of diversity in publishing and the arts more generally makes this particularly important. For a white writer to attempt to articulate the perspective of a person of colour is clearly undesirable given the profound lack of representation of historically oppressed people on publishers' lists: the diversification of stories without the diversification of the voices telling them perpetuates inequality. If fiction, like acting, relies on the communication of 'authentic emotions' under 'imagined circumstances', it cannot function unless the author can recall and empathise with the feelings they are trying to convey. This criticism was levelled at Jeanine Cummins for her controversial novel *American Dirt,*[31] in which Cummins, a white woman, tells the story of two Mexican migrants trying to cross the border into the US. Cummins' defence was that she aimed to humanise people whom she claimed, to much ire, are often imagined as 'a faceless brown mass'.[32] Yet by recounting an experience she could not possibly fully understand, it's difficult to see how she could do anything but perpetuate this problem for her audiences – not least because it was *her* face that ended up splashed across outraged media.

A secondary problem is that even if one accepts that writing what you know is a fair limitation that prevents naive writers from perpetuating stereotypes or taking up valuable space, it also limits other writers. If writing about a particular identity is confined to those with first-hand experience of its impact, those people risk being pigeonholed into 'identity writing'. Monica Ali, who has Bangladeshi heritage, received a lukewarm response to the novels that followed her debut hit, *Brick Lane,* and lost confidence, resolving never to write again. She told the *Times* in early 2022 that she sensed this was because the other material was somehow not 'authentic' enough. 'A few people have asked me, were you trying to get away from *Brick Lane*? What would that have been? My ethnicity? No, how could I? Why would I want to?' she said. 'Where I was stupid and naive was thinking that I could write about anything I wanted to write about, that I had as much right to do that as a white male writer.'[33]

*

There is perhaps no stronger relationship between the artist and its perceivers than in pop music, where a universal 'I' abounds. Because of its close ties to celebrity culture, pop stars are also subject to even greater scrutiny over their 'authenticity' – as people and as artists. Although fiction has greater scope to commentate openly on itself than perhaps any other art form, in pop we also witness the construction of personas that enable audiences to lose – and subsequently find – themselves in someone else.

Because music is so immersive and mystical, artists can encourage listeners to become unfixed by nurturing a consistent, holistic 'vibe': the strength of the vibe functions as a stand-in for authenticity, connoting a powerful personal brand. By the time Lana Del Rey released her sixth studio album *Norman Fucking Rockwell!* (*NFR*) in 2019, she was known not just for her voice (syrupy and sarcastic), nor for her music (glossy and melancholic), but for her overall aesthetic: an F. Scott Fitzgerald love interest in low-rise jeans. Since *Born to Die,* her second album and first major success, Del Rey has captured elusive emotions such as nostalgia and longing using what feel like highly specific image references. She seems to have become a symbol for symbolism itself. What Lana Del Rey has 'invented', according to various Twitter users, could be made into a fascinating museum display; following the release of *NFR,* one viral tweet from a fan account listed them to include cocaine, 'your dad', the USA national anthem, 'the gays who scam rich men', old men, everything cherry-flavoured, cigarettes, sex, and the iPhone 6s+.[34]

Lana Del Rey's layered references, sensory invocations and doubling down on her own image show that a kind of post-authentic metafiction can also be written through pop music. This is a field where persona is paramount. But perhaps because in pop music the artist has always embodied just as much for fans as the art, authenticity – that is, an intense presentation of self – is equally prized. In a review of *NFR,* the music critic Ann Powers noted that in Del Rey's early career, 'intimations that she'd had help in inventing herself clouded her status'.[35] It was only once she was able to encase her pastiche into her authentic self that she and her music began to provide the collective euphoria that only a special kind of pop can induce.

Trilling writes that for the modernists, 'the poet is not a person at all, only a *persona*'.[36] The lack of the artist's true self within a work does not preclude an authentic experience for the reader or listener. In fact, it can increase it. Powers wrote in her *NFR* review that 'this is not only about Del Rey's persona as a bad girl to whom bad things are done; her supposed confessions would be nothing more than reality-show fodder if not for the way she and her collaborators construct them';[37] that 'her pastiche is so perfectly constructed it becomes flesh'.[38] And yet this seeming accusation of inauthenticity – despite the fact Powers was actually praising Del Rey for her skill – incited defensiveness in Del Rey herself. 'Here's a little sidenote on your piece. I don't even relate to one observation you made about the music,' she wrote on Twitter. 'There's nothing uncooked about me. To write about me is nothing like it is to be with me. Never had a persona. Never needed one. Never will.'[39]

This outright rejection of the idea of 'persona' is perhaps because we learned in the early 2010s that musical authenticity looked like a total lack of one. The rise in the early 2010s of what Radio 1's Chris Price called 'acoustic-guitar-wielding troubadours',[40] following the dulcet suburban tones of late 2000s indie and inspired by the enormous success of Ed Sheeran, represented a drive for authenticity in the music industry. Sheeran pioneered a specific type of ordinary-guy pop that soared as a result of its low-key relatability – it was all jeans and T-shirts, VO5 and kissing in car parks, not to mention sonically stripped-back. It was clear to labels that Sheeran had touched on something golden: he was able to speak to the masses without any obvious pretence or theatre. It was perfect for them – there was no need for pyrotechnics or dancers, you just put him on stage with a loop pedal and let him sing – and perfect for the audience, too, arriving as it did at the end of a decade of autotune, bands manufactured on talent shows, and authenticity anxiety that left people clamouring for someone they could trust.

But that Sheeran and his imitators (such as Rag n Bone Man, Tom Grennan and Louis Capaldi) looked like your mate from the pub didn't necessarily mean their characters were any less artfully constructed. They, and their songs, were simply more easily relatable than the pearlescent nostalgia created by Del Rey or the saccharine escapism of, say, One Direction. In all kinds of pop music, as with self-baring autofiction, the listener can become absorbed by someone else's world – it's just when that world is Ed Sheeran's, it looks like a date night at Cineworld, and when it's Lana Del Rey's, it looks like a 1950s erotic thriller. If there is no familiarity, its appeal must be in the escape it offers: the music must be powerful enough that we almost believe these could be our real feelings.

It seems that, like reality TV stars, musical artists are increasingly inclined to fold into their act the process of creating their own persona. The Disney Channel star Olivia Rodrigo has been accused of plagiarism multiple times – and yet her constructed character is strong enough that the perceived truthfulness of her work has been relatively unaffected. Though she was a child star, and has an establishment background, she conveys a general sense of authenticity. In the video for her debut hit 'drivers license',[41] for example, she is dressed in ordinary, casual outfits. She is singing about

51

heartbreak. The song's title is presented in slapdash online vernacular: all lower-case and with a missing apostrophe, seemingly taken directly from a teaser clip of the song on Rodrigo's Instagram in 2020, in the caption of which she wrote 'gonna call it drivers license I think lol'.[42]

Rodrigo is, to put it generously, candid about her inspirations, visual and musical. The songs on *Sour*, the album that followed 'drivers license' in May 2021, are at times almost indistinguishable from the work of Taylor Swift or Lorde. The video for 'good 4 u'[43] is a showreel of visual pop culture references, parodying *The Princess Diaries* and *Jennifer's Body* and music videos by Michael Jackson, Britney, and Swift again, a cocktail of Noughties nostalgia. The music is heavily inspired by turn-of-the-century pop-punk, and builds on the shoulders of Gen-Z star Billie Eilish. Rodrigo appears to be unflinching in revealing the conditions of her work's construction. Even within the first few seconds of *Sour*, there is a spoken line, designed to sound throwaway, that situates the listener in her process: 'I want it to be, like, messy'.[44] Why not just make it, like, messy? Why tell us as much? Because, in blatantly revealing the self of the author, not just the author's artistic voice, Rodrigo earns our trust. If pop is fiction, she is not just writing autofiction – she is writing metafiction.

*

At the end of *Trust Exercise*, we turn the page to Choi's acknowledgements. 'Writing fiction is like dreaming,' she writes; 'the recognisable and the unthinkable... coalesce in the least predictable ways, in the end turning into something entirely unlike real life, and yet hopefully relevant in some way to our shared human life.'[45] Choi herself attended a specialist theatre school in her teens. The extent to which the circumstances of the novel as a whole, and Sarah and Karen's stories within it, are 'imagined' is ambiguous. *Trust Exercise* is, of course, the ultimate trust exercise for the reader: it constantly undermines its own reality; points out the untrustworthiness of its own narrators; proves itself to straddle that boundary between the recognisable and unthinkable – between reality and unreality.

Its liminality exposes our anxiety to fix artistic works within the spectrum of real to imagined. Perhaps it is easier for us to relinquish control and submit to our own prospective fluidity as readers or listeners by first understanding how much control the author has over their own self as it manifests in the work. There is a power dynamic at play: we increasingly resist the author's hold on our authentic emotions unless they are also giving part of themselves to us.

PRODUCT

Consider the hipster: in his truest form, he floats somewhere between 2000 and 2012, is aged between 25 and 35,
and lives in London, Berlin or a major US city. He is white,
but he could be of virtually any build, height or hair colour.
His distinctive features are cultivated: he has a beard that is
tamed using oil explicitly made for that purpose; he wears
thick-rimmed glasses, which may or may not aid his vision.
His denim is raw; his ankles are bare; his tote bag is hemp.
He drinks artisanal coffee and craft beer and listens only to
vinyl records in certain genres: including, but not limited
to, jazz fusion, folk and anything that is from (or sounds
vaguely like it's from) the 1970s. He has an iconographic
tattoo on his bicep that was acquired some years ago and
is source material for self-deprecation (it is usually visible
anyway). He is considering another, maybe just a shape this
time. He works in 'the creative industries', which could mean
anything from actual art to the media to writing slogans for

multivitamin adverts. It doesn't really matter because we understand that what he means by this is that he is himself a creative, which is to say he has a humanities degree. His flat has some combination of exposed wood floors, a framed French film poster, a Japanese tea set and a warehouse vibe.

The emergence of the hipster at this time was not a coincidence. From the late 1990s, collective anxiety surrounding authenticity had increased as Silicon Valley began to explode with innovation and the new millennium crackled with the potential for dystopia. In his 2003 book *Authenticity,*[1] the British business and economics writer David Boyle wrote fervently of the importance of authenticity in a world where people watched sunsets through video cameras and brands used rebellion as a selling point. Performative, corporate authenticity – such as when, in the aftermath of the 1999 anti-globalisation protests in Seattle surrounding the World Trade Organisation conference, Gap decorated their shop fronts across the world with graffiti – is 'fake-real', Boyle suggests: 'Real experience has depth. It is more than just a superficial engagement with a brand.'[2]

Hipsterism – a term that has been used to describe self-consciously trendy types for decades but came to define a specific kind of middle-class, bespectacled, fixed-gear-bike-riding Shoreditch-dweller in the 2000s – was similarly a confused combination of materialism and anti-establishment cool, in which you had to be seen to be going against the grain but where the primary means of doing so was buying more stuff. A personal sense of authenticity had to be propped up by authentic products.

In its 2000s form, hipsterism prized graininess, artisanship and alternatives to the mainstream. It was contrived bohemianism but hipsters thought they were partaking in an authentic counterculture – that they had found the analogue antidote to the banality and artificiality of mass culture and new technology. The onslaught of manufactured pop was mitigated by returning to vinyl; listening to music on MP3 players was counteracted by wearing cassette tapes as necklaces. That these mini rebellions manifested in nostalgia was partly an attempt to escape the present moment, but the obsession with traditional media like vinyl records and film cameras was also about getting to the real essence of an experience – the most authentic way of listening to music or taking pictures. 'Third wave' coffee, the hipster's preferred method of caffeination, was about extracting the maximum flavour from specially roasted fairtrade coffee beans using state-of-the-art equipment, a process that was almost insurgent against mass-producing them in a factory and then bastardising them in a Frappuccino, and which professed to be the quintessential experience of consuming coffee. It's also no coincidence that hipsters tended to be deeply pessimistic about the state of things as they were; it was cool to hate everything, but it was also reasonable. New Labour? *The X Factor*? Facebook, but no dislike button? Polaroids and vintage cardigans provided hope of salvation.

Now, though, when we cackle maniacally at one another online before 9 a.m. by writing the word 'SCREAMING' or an extended 'haha' with just enough mistakes for everyone to know that we are too busy laughing to bother typing correctly; when teenagers make pocket money by creating memes, or modelling and selling 'rare' Brandy Melville tops on Depop; and when our desire for soya-based custard, freshly made sushi or a chocolate milkshake can in urban areas be met within 15 minutes via an app and a gig-economy worker on an electric scooter, earnest concerns about the takeover of mass culture almost feel retro. There are still 'hipsters' – people who think they're cooler than everyone else – but their identity no longer rests so fundamentally on this specific conception of 'authenticity'.

This is partly because the popularity of the hipster aesthetic, ironically, only further entrenched performed authenticity as 'fake real'. M&S, for example, still puts pornographic close-ups of cheesecake on TV to make it clear its food is something we could touch and taste, not just see pictures of. Further culinary options include Huel, a nutritional smoothie that essentially allows us to elide the experience of eating while still ingesting food's necessary qualities; organic small plates restaurants, which, by using 'seasonal, local produce' and by writing a menu so pure and uncorrupted that we have to take a substantial leap of faith when ordering (choosing between 'Curds, fennel' and 'Ox cheek, swede'), fetishise the granular authenticity of the dining experience to the point of parody; and McDonald's, which advertises itself as a no-nonsense, anti-hipster paradise to have a chat with your mates. In other words, weaponising symbolic authenticity for marketing is such standard practice with so many iterations that perhaps we simply no longer notice – or care.

Yet it has undeniably evolved to evade world-weary cynicism. Authenticity is appealing partly because of its elusiveness. It is a perfectly unattainable attribute that sustains desire. And so, brands have learned that they must sell us more than their authentic products. They must attempt to sell us a version of our authentic selves.

*

Symbolic authenticity has always been important to brands. In the late nineteenth century, when the Industrial Revolution started to create distinct production houses for certain goods, distributors began to add logos to their products that were often designed to appear rustic and familiar, reassuring the consumer they were buying something well-made and personal. As businesses multiplied and counterfeit models proliferated, marketing explicitly on authenticity was a way of saying you were getting the real deal – and that the brand was not trying to swindle you. This is the most basic definition of authenticity: proving a product is consistent on the inside and outside – a premise epitomised in Ronseal's 1994 advert for floor varnish, which simply promised that the product 'does exactly what it says on the tin'.[3]

Technological revolution and globalisation heightened the stakes for brand authenticity. Unease had arisen in the West after decades of developing capitalism and peaked in the late 1990s, on the cusp of a new century. The sense of anxiety surrounding digitisation, virtual reality and the looming future of the new millennium was explored in popular films of the time: *The Matrix* and *The Truman Show* both depicted false realities created to hide a stark dystopia and control the real, human characters within them.

If authenticity was supposed to appear to be an antidote to capitalism, it was no longer enough for companies to stick a homely looking label on a jam jar – discerning consumers would recognise the strategy instantly as 'fake real'. Rather, as Naomi Klein wrote in *No Logo* in 1999, 'successful corporations must primarily produce brands, as opposed to products'.[4] The 'authenticity' of brands was not simply about whether their products matched their marketed description or offered an earthy or ethical experience, but whether the brand had created a sufficiently consistent and genuine-seeming identity. Klein wrote that 'if a brand was not a product, it could be anything'.[5] A brand, then, could be held to the same standards of 'authenticity' as human beings – and for human beings, authenticity meant self-realisation.

Just as brands became approximations of people, people began to turn into approximations of brands. During the 2000s, as social media boomed and the markets crashed, there was a dawning sense that we could, or should, commodify ourselves. But such a process required more commodities in turn: products are not simply objects that serve their immediate purpose but identity markers that reflect on or appear to improve us as people: buying a particular product does not merely result in your owning the product but in your being the type of person who has chosen to do so. Trinkets coveted by hipsters were 'authentic' in their own right in that they were vintage or handmade, but they also made their owners appear authentic because they differentiated them from the mass-produced mainstream. By surrounding themselves with the right things, hipsters appeared to be forging an original path and building a genuine identity guided by the inner self – or perhaps just a consistent personal brand to be marketed back to an audience.

That hipsterism was a phenomenon adopted almost exclusively by the white middle classes did little to enhance its reputation. Its particular way of demonstrating authentic personhood mainly involved being wealthy and educated enough to buy the 'right' things. Hipsters gentrified urban areas and looked down on people they perceived to be uncool with little consideration of whether they could afford to appear any differently. They were, stereotypically, politically ambivalent: educated enough to know things were bad, but sufficiently distanced from difficulty not to care. (This phenomenon, of course, still occurs, even if the 'right' things are now slightly different and 'hipster' is no longer such a specific category.)

Once hipsterism became a parody of itself, functioning on the same values of 'authenticity' as the brands it intended to counteract, it also became a paradox. By the late 2000s Urban Outfitters was fully stocked with record players and vintage-looking knitwear. Suburban teenage girls appropriating hipster style via multinational corporations enraged nobody more than the hipsters themselves, but by then it was too late. The model was copied over and over again until it was impossible to distinguish which was the original iteration and which was a facsimile. First-generation hipsters may well have authentically hated Pizza Express and adored their flat's proximity to Hackney Wick, but no amount of protestation or extra detail could (by around 2012) outweigh the fact that they looked and sounded exactly like a run-of-the-mill dickhead.[6]

*

Starbucks, a chain coffee shop with over 32,000 stores in more than 80 countries worldwide, seems like a textbook example of an 'inauthentic' brand. Its pumpkin spice macchiatos, toffee nut cappuccinos, chestnut praline mochas and eggnog lattes are anathema to the hipster's single-origin cold brew. It is ubiquitous at airports and service stations and known for serving its drinks in branded half-litre cups. Yet this hasn't always been the case. Starbucks was once held up as the opposite: a brand for whom an authentic atmosphere was of paramount importance and whose brand essence was prioritised over the specificities of its products.

In 1997, then-CEO Howard Schultz wrote in his brand-story book *Pour Your Heart Into It* that people went to Starbucks for the 'romance of the experience'.[7] Scott Bedbury, Starbucks' VP of marketing, said, 'consumers don't truly believe there's a huge difference between products'.[8] And so instead of products per se, Starbucks nurtured a vibe – one that sold you both the experience of being there and the promise of rubbing off on you after you'd walked out the door. Going to Starbucks wasn't just about drinking coffee or sitting in a very low armchair under slightly dimmed lighting, pretending to read – it was about being seen there, or walking around with the logo-stamped cup as an accessory. Its cool, casually wasteful frivolity told people something about who you were (somebody sufficiently flush to spend £2.50 on a coffee and too busy and important to sit down and drink it). When Starbucks opened in my small Suffolk hometown in around 2009 the cosmopolitan glamour of buying a caramel cream Frappuccino after school – despite any hipster advice to the contrary – was unprecedented.

As Starbucks continued to expand, making headlines about workers' rights and gaining a reputation for being 'on every corner' in London, it was soon maligned as an inauthentic multinational. But almost as quickly as it fell from grace – and *because* it fell from grace – Starbucks began to symbolise authenticity in a new way: it was 'basic'.

The 'basic bitch' evolved from a term of derision to empowerment over the first half of the 2010s, in correlation with the hipster's demise and the more general rise of 'poptimism', in which pop culture started to be considered to be as worthy of analysis and as serious as high culture. To call someone 'basic' is snooty and mean. It means somebody is a philistine, too easily pleased by the popular and too stupid or uninteresting to understand the higher intellectual or cultural plane inhabited by the person saying it. Noreen Malone wrote in a 2014 piece for *The Cut*:

> [W]hile what it pretends to criticize is unoriginality of thought and action, most of what *basic* actually seeks to dismiss is consumption patterns – what you watch, what

63

you drink, what you wear, and what you buy – without dismissing consumption itself. The basic girl's sin isn't liking to shop, it's cluelessly lusting after the wrong brands.[9]

Crucially, both basicness and criticism of basicness are rooted in consumerism. But the basic bitch is unaware of herself, while the hipster or the snob is painfully aware of the implications for his own identity of everything he buys.

However, while true basicness manifests in 'cluelessly' buying all the wrong things, it is something entirely different to own, to author, one's basicness. As 'authenticity' became mainstream and hipsterism more obviously pretentious than ever, owning up to being basic – by, for example, posting a picture of your pumpkin spice latte on Instagram and captioning it #basicbitch – emerged as socially rebellious (all the more so because for all their brand-awareness, true hipsters also lacked *self*-awareness: as another *Cut* article from 2014 had it, they have 'never heard of hipsters and likely wouldn't understand the definition').[10]

It wasn't just as an antidote to hipster culture that basicness took on this quality. Consumer habits with the reputation for being basic – like consuming pop culture, wearing mass-produced clothing and, yes, going to Starbucks – were also associated with feminine, LGBTQ or working-class cultures; being interested in makeup, sincerely enjoying Eurovision, or going on a package holiday to Marbella also once may have been described as 'basic' (such preferences have since been wrapped up in the altogether more accepting world of 'hun' culture). Reclaiming these products or hobbies as legitimate ways to spend money and time pushed back against the sense that you weren't allowed, as someone in one of those often maligned identity groups, just to like what you liked – even if what you liked involved indulging in a little consumerist amorality.

So hipsterism declined because its 'authenticity' began to seem inauthentic, and the 'inauthenticity' of the basic bitch, and her pop culture preferences, started to seem authentic as a result – proving that the moment you begin to perform authenticity, it becomes meaningless. Yet authenticity begins to crumble *without* self-awareness, too: how can you know you're living as your true self if you simply conform unthinkingly to mainstream interests? What's more, what if – either by rejecting what's popular or leaning into it – your authenticity is cultivated for the sake of it? Does that still count – are you still being yourself?

*

The philosopher and psychologist William James wrote in 1890 that 'a man's Self is the sum total of all that he can call his' – including 'his clothes and his house… his yacht and his bank account'.[11] If this is the case, then our sense of who we are has since been challenged and confused by a drastically inflated level of choice surrounding what we can buy. This is why branding is so important: distinguishing between products is difficult, but feeling the vibe of a brand is easy. Rather than choosing between a seemingly endless array of different types of the same product, we simply have to choose a brand with which to associate ourselves based on which best reflects who we are on the inside.

This process of positive association with products is replicated within brands themselves via celebrity partnerships. They associate themselves with the right person and become synonymous with whatever that person stands for. Nike's sponsorship of Michael Jordan, one of the best-known brand partnerships of all time, was successful not least because the first edition of Air Jordan trainers came, in 1984, with a healthy dose of authentic rebellion. Jordan was initially supposed to wear the shoes during matches. The NBA prohibited him from doing so because of their colour scheme – but he was still in Nike's adverts. As Jordan, standing stationary against a blank background and glistening with sweat, slowly dribbles a basketball and passes it between his hands, each bounce echoing, an official-sounding male voice says: 'On September 15, Nike created a revolutionary new basketball shoe. On October 18, the NBA threw them out of the game. Fortunately, the NBA can't keep you from wearing them.'[12] Over the following two years, Air Jordans generated over $100 million in sales (the equivalent of $255 million today).[13]

Jordan's partnership with Nike was mutually beneficial. Not only did it make both parties money, but it enhanced each of their identities. It increased Jordan's visibility as an up-and-coming star; for Nike – which at the time was 50 per cent smaller than Adidas in terms of revenue and, before the Air Jordans came out, much less popular than Converse among basketball players – Jordan refreshed their image, giving them something specific to pin themselves to. Suddenly, their market encompassed everyone who was a fan of MJ – which, a couple of years later, was not just basketball fans but pretty much everybody.

Not all celebrity brand partnerships are, of course, as successful as Michael Jordan and Nike's. In fact, appearing in advertising campaigns as a celebrity can equally be a surefire way to signify outright inauthenticity and make everyone think you have 'sold out'. Iggy Pop's Swiftcover car insurance ad in 2009 did little for his street cred, particularly when it emerged that Swiftcover does not provide insurance for entertainers and was banned on the grounds of being misleading. Jennifer Lopez's supposedly authentic Fiat advert, in which she appeared to be driving through the Bronx in New York ('the block' she was famously from), was mocked: it was actually filmed against a green screen in LA.

Today, being a celebrity brand endorser is a viable career path in itself. For an aspiring influencer, the goal is to have enough followers that brands want to pay you to showcase their products, and then to accumulate more followers as a result of the products you showcase. This 'human billboard' marketing model, which has developed over the past few years to encompass ongoing partnerships and business deals for big-hitting influencers, continues to proliferate. In 2020 the number of brand-sponsored posts uploaded to Instagram had almost doubled in two years to 6.1 million.[14] Just like the traditional celebrity partnership, the influencer-brand partnership is symbiotic: being paid to showcase certain products contributes to your own personal brand.

Yet the influencing model has also diverged from the traditional celebrity partnership. Being the face of brands is the primary income stream of an influencer, whereas for celebrities advertising augments (or hopes to revive) a career elsewhere. And, at least in influencers' original iteration, the reason they were effective for brands was precisely the opposite of celebrities' stardust: influencers were ordinary.

*

Social media influencing has become the ultimate commodification of self, distilling personhood and lifestyle into a consistent essence and then advertising this essence in its own right. Influencers are not only ambassadors for brands and products: they are themselves brands and products. This means that they are held to the same standards of 'authenticity' as brands and products. Yet a decade after influencing emerged as an industry in its own right, it would be reasonable to say that this commodification is widely viewed as inherently inauthentic – that the process of inflating and monetising the self negates any sense of the ordinariness that was once the point.

As it does celebrity, a fractious combination of fake and real defines the world of influencing, which now comprises a significant proportion of the advertising industry. Social media is built on a foundation of selectiveness: it is necessarily both withholding and giving. The curation of a feed allows the user to project exactly the image they want people to see but also requires them to expose themselves to judgement.

For professional influencers, there is also the question of how up-front you are about your motives: should you appear to be authentically an influencer, brazenly flogging whatever makes you rich quickest, or authentically yourself, retaining the influencer's unique selling point – a just-like-you relatability – and making the strategically placed products look like an afterthought?

The specific question of influencer inauthenticity arose in the mid-2010s, almost as soon as influencers had fully entered the mainstream, when it became apparent that they were covertly being paid for posts that were made to look like snapshots of their real lives. In 2018 the Advertising Standards Agency introduced legislation that meant influencers had to come clean if a post was set up as an ad, or if it featured a product 'gifted' to them by the brand for free with the hope of promotion. Suddenly the industry was busted: legally, influencers could no longer pretend that their picture-perfect holiday was simply a mysterious, fortuitous occurrence in their already picture-perfect life when in fact the hotel had paid for them to go.

The embarrassment inherent in celebrity adverts such as Iggy Pop's and J.Lo's stems from the exposure of their needing the brand as much as the brand needs them. Similarly, the legislation forced influencers to admit perhaps the most inauthentic trait of all: that they needed money. We aspire to celebrities' and influencers' lifestyles partly because they seem effortless: they are somehow able to live luxuriously, unperturbed by trivial worries such as rent. In *Authenticity*, Boyle noted the 'all-pervasive belief that somehow we are only living authentically when we're not working',[15] an idea that both propelled and was capitalised on by the tourism industry in the early 2000s. Rather than holidays being a way to escape the sobering 'reality' of working life, he writes that 'reality is when we are resting or travelling. Or when we're drunk, or high, or canoeing, or halfway up a mountain in a blizzard'.[16] Influencers similarly attempt to perform a particularly aspirational kind of truth-living that makes their lives seem like they're all play. Otherwise, nobody would want to be them.

Although within the industry brand partnerships bolster, rather than undermine, the legitimacy of influencers (aspiring influencers are known to post fake sponsored content to seem more credible and established to other prospective brand-partners), this is not because there is anything in the act of selling products that is inherently authentic. As much as influencers like to be transparent about their lives and proud of their skills, and no matter how cool they are or how legitimate the brand they are flogging, the '#ad' at the end of immaculately crafted captions on beautiful, effortless-seeming photos is still, somehow, disruptive to the overall image. Organic food and artisan furniture became panicked, clearly insufficient antidotes to the threats of genetic modification and automation in the 2000s; now, the idea of an authentic self defined by joy (good) prevails as the antithesis of an inauthentic self defined by work (bad). Of course, this is a highly privileged position, a fantasy of those for whom attaining a self without work and wages is even imaginable. There is a sense that for those for whom it is not, it is acceptable for the self to become bound up with their work because it confers a certain grit – a struggle almost as enviably authentic as lifestyles that have none whatsoever.

*

The world of influencing endures. In 2022, the industry was worth \$16.4bn, almost double its value in 2020.[17] A US survey in 2020 showed that 61 per cent of consumers trusted product recommendations from influencers – compared to 38 per cent who trusted direct marketing from a brand – and 82 per cent had purchased or researched a product after seeing it recommended on social media.[18] We know this is an industry designed to make us part with our money more readily, yet we don't seem to mind.

Aside from our hardened, weary outlook on capitalism, this is because influencers are selling us more products that serve their purpose as objects – more, even, than themselves as desirable brands. They are selling a *sense* of self. In showing us their lives, which are necessarily beautiful enough to put online, we are given an example of how to be ourselves, too. If brands once consciously switched to becoming more like a person with an inner self, influencers have reappropriated this brand-self hybrid for themselves – a person with an inner self becomes a brand with an inner self who then markets themselves as a person again. Having moved through this authenticity-making machine, the lives they put online are two steps removed from real life. The result is something their followers – whose subjective experience is, naturally,

71

firmly rooted in their own real life – can observe and try to emulate. The effect of influencers' impeccable personal brands is not only for followers to think '*I want to be you*', but to ask: '*How can I be as much me as you are you?*'

Products are often instruments for cultivating a sense of self, too. While brands have historically tried to push the idea that their products will help you transcend, or at least improve, the self, in contemporary consumerism they are rarely so bold as to assume you have anything to improve on at all, instead resorting to platitudes about individual empowerment that often make the role of their product unclear. Invoking authenticity in this way has a particularly stringent effect on the beauty industry. It is taboo to tell people they should change themselves to be more beautiful, which means that beauty products can only be sold on the basis that the consumer is already beautiful. Naturally, this undermines much of the purpose of beauty products, but new language covers it. Many products now enhance and define rather than cover or create. The rise of the specialised skincare industry, which by 2021 made up 27 per cent of the beauty industry overall, marks a subtle shift in consumer interests. Deciem, the Canadian skincare brand that owns millennial cult favourite The Ordinary, has had enormous success by selling itself on clinical specificities. This has led to an influx of similar products across the industry. Consumers seek out specific ingredients – vitamin C for 'energising', hyaluronic acid for 'hydrating' – rather than being led by the vague spin of an advertising campaign or grand promises made on a bottle. This is brand authenticity, of course – The Ordinary is careful to keep its packaging monochrome and clinical, as straight-up and scientific as it comes – but it also offers self-improvement without compromising self-authenticity.[19]

Brands have simply replaced making us feel inadequate with making us feel confused. In this climate of turbo-positivity, where we are bombarded with companies saying, with a slightly manic air, 'You're great as you are!' next to a picture of their product, it's difficult to know what to think or do. If I'm good enough as I am, why would I need to buy this product specifically? Am I not good enough to make myself feel good enough on my own, with the things I already have? And what if I don't feel good enough? Am I allowed to change what's natural to make myself feel better? I want this moisturiser, and I'm sad, so I deserve a treat, but because I'm sad, I also shouldn't give in to the pressure to conform to conventional beauty standards that said moisturiser would provide to me. Should I subtly tweak the pH balance of my cheeks for £32 per 30ml because it will make me more of the self I already am?

*

Symbolic authenticity as a basic brand value continues to hold mainstream importance. McDonald's' recent advertising campaigns have depicted it as a warm, welcoming place and emphasised their no-fuss, anti-hipster attitude to coffee. A slightly condescending TV ad for Moretti beer – an Italian lager owned by Heineken – shows people in a cheerful, rustic Italian village sharing the beer together, in

Italian, with subtitles; Moretti's tagline is *'Birra autentica'*. Authentic-seeming products are still coveted, perhaps, because of continuing capitalist globalisation and the disconnect between the items in our hands and their centre of production. Clothing-brand authenticity is conveyed more than ever with 'transparency' about how and where its products are made due to public concern about the climate emergency and the appalling humanitarian conditions for garment workers in South Asia. Just as brand ethics was in the 1990s, this is reduced to signalling and performance, with the mere presence of a 'climate policy' or 'product journey' on a brand's website reassuring the consumer that it's all being taken care of, while murky practices down the supply chain continue to occur.

Beyond these attempts to position themselves as unique, ethical and 'genuine', brands also attempt to cultivate personhood online. As people have become shinier, brands have ostensibly got rougher: they post memes and engage in affected banter with competitors as though they were both humans. A social media assistant sitting at their desk attempting to channel the authentic voice of the disembodied entity that pays their rent is supposed to give the brand an online identity that makes it appear to have an inner life. It might be hard and shiny on the outside, but it's soft in the middle, just like the rest of us.

In 2022 a TV advert for the Google Pixel phone ended with the slogan: 'The things that make you who you are make this phone what it is'. All roads lead back to this, the sense of self. We are guided by that second layer of authenticity: not

74

just what we want, but what will make us more ourselves. Not just what we practically need, but what the person we are inside desperately yearns for. Where once there were clear divisions between what we perceived as authentic and inauthentic products – artisanal vs mass-produced; hipster vs basic – now there is only the self. Our consumption habits reflect what Charles Taylor describes as 'the liberalism of neutrality'.[20] If we champion unadulterated authenticity – that is, every individual living out their unique truth – we cannot be prescriptive about what constitutes a good life, aesthetically or morally. The Starbucks Frappuccino and the artisan flat white are equally weighted until you tip the scales.

If the only cultural and political value attributed to our consumer choices is simply whether or not they are consistent with our personal preference, how do we hold brands accountable for anything? And where does this leave those who do not have endless options – who cannot afford to follow their 'authentic' desires? If we define selfhood by what we own, the selfhood of people who own less or cannot own what they truly desire is undermined. Even for those with the resources, it is impossible to weigh up all the options in a swarm of seemingly infinite choice. The authentic option may not present itself. We have to know who we are already.

Yet just when you think you do, you see an advert.

Want to be a better version of you?

The doubt sets in. *Maybe that's who I am. Maybe that's what I want.*

What do you want? What do you want? What do you want?

75

IDENTITY

What's the difference between politics and identity politics? The most politically significant events of the past century have concerned gender, race, class, religion, sexuality and nationhood. Identity affects all of us – gives us meaning, helps us to connect with others and to find our place in the world – and so it is necessarily embedded in democracy. And yet when we talk about 'identity politics' we tend to mean something specific: divided, tribal culture wars in which we struggle to speak productively about identity and in which invoking it is viewed either as a failsafe argument-winner or as an overly emotional excuse for dodging the real questions. This breakdown in communication – and the rhetorical tipping of politics into much maligned 'identity politics' – is caused by our obsession with authenticity.

The 'inner self' and the sanctity of the individual have never been held in greater significance. And yet identity is at least partly about a tangible outer self, too – one that is part of a collective. 'Identifying' with a particular social group allows us to tether the 'true self', which is slippery and elusive, to a set of fixed characteristics. An identity gives us the vocabulary and the tools to perform our selfhood – to say 'this is who I am'. Identity and authenticity are all too easy to conflate, but the crucial differences between them create a discourse in which selfishness and empathy, feeling and fact, are often confused.

To point out the problems with popularised contemporary 'identity politics' is not to diminish its importance for marginalised people. The movement of the last decade, much of which has taken place online, has helped to liberate many people from oppressive dynamics and systems. Yet where identity politics should start with the self and end with the collective, using unique experience to identify and address structural issues, too often in contemporary culture do we witness people – most often, it is worth saying, not those from marginalised groups – utilising the collective to benefit the self.

It is also important to recognise that 'pure' authenticity – which is traditionally represented by a self liberated from societal pressures – is only possible to project from a position of substantial privilege. Someone who is perceived to be living their full, unattached 'best life' is likely to conform to Western ideals that free them from first being noticed for, or perceived as synonymous with, their race, appearance or any other attribute. If you are the societal default, you are free to roam and be 'authentic'. Conversely, if you are in the minority in any given context, you are much more likely to be defined by your identity. And the more you are labelled as a particular thing by the outside world, on whatever scale and whether or not that label causes oppression, the less you are able to have what you feel is your true inner self recognised by others.

In this way, a tension arises between defining the boundaries of identity and liberating people from them – between being recognised *for* your identity and despite it. William Davies wrote in the *London Review of Books* in 2021 that identity politics concerns 'the right [of people] to define themselves on their own terms and refuse to be defined according to official or expert classifications'.[1] In *Identity* Francis Fukuyama writes that identity politics is about the struggle for dignity, which is ultimately the right to exist as an individual free of any constraints imposed on your identity group.[2] Equally, identity is something 'assigned to a person by members of his group', according to Alvin W Gouldner, an early scholar of the idea of a 'social identity'. 'They observe or impute to a person certain characteristics,' Gouldner writes; 'they observe certain aspects of his behaviour or appearance which they employ as clues to enable themselves to answer the question "Who is he?"'.[3] Similarly, our sense of our own identity is only available when we think of our lives in the third person. And while Davies' and Fukuyama's idea of the *right* to self-definition is not in direct contravention of being categorised externally at the same time, as the establishment of both individual and collective truth grows in cultural importance it is easy to see how each tangles and smothers the other's meaning.

The climate of fear frequently weaponised in conservative media as 'cancel culture', or 'woke', liberal 'snowflakes' policing the behaviour of ordinary people is a direct result of this confusion. If the inner self and identity are viewed as synonymous, a comment on the collective can feel like an attack on an individual, and genuinely racist or misogynistic sentiment can be framed as legitimate criticism of one person. Nowhere is this more evident than in the frequent justification of the abuse directed towards the black MP Diane Abbott as harmless, even necessary, political commentary.

The search for an identity is not a way of dodging the search for authenticity. It simply applies the flawed framework of authenticity to something outside the self. The problem is that authenticity is tethered to unique, individual experience: it represents something true, but true specifically for one person, while within a collective, there has to be room for more than one truth. Is it possible for these two ideas to co-exist?

*

The psychoanalyst Erik Erikson coined the term 'identity crisis' in his book *Childhood and Society*[4] to explain a period of confusion in adolescence about the direction of one's life – a confusion that Erikson himself had experienced. Erikson's 'identity confusion' stemmed from his being tall, blonde-haired and blue-eyed – his father was Danish – but spending his adolescence living with his Jewish stepfather in southwest Germany. He was called '*goy*' ('non-Jew') in his stepfather's community and 'Jew' at school.

Erikson's experience demonstrates how identity is both at odds with and dependent on authenticity. A social identity is, as Stuart Hall has put it, a 'collective "one true self"'.[5] That Erikson did not fit easily into either category illustrates how authenticity is demanded of social identities such as these: the collective must realise what their true self is, just as individuals do, and then make sure any entry to the group is based on those criteria. The outward definition of the group becomes dependent on the inner definition, and vice versa.

This essentialism is what makes so-called identity politics divisive: it naturally invites exclusiveness. You are only allowed to 'identify' as part of a group if you meet specific criteria – Erikson was neither a Jew nor a non-Jew. The more selective the criteria, the more ostracised people who don't meet or understand it feel. Increasingly complex definitions of sexuality, for example, may send *Daily Mail* readers on an anti-woke rampage simply because they do not understand the definition of – or the point of defining – certain identities. This does not diminish the importance, to the people who identify as such, of putting a name to their experience (whether they want to do so to realise their inner selves or whether it is useful for a broader collective or political aim). Indeed, it probably increases it.

Authenticity is key here. The integrity of the authentic collective self means that those who seek to be granted entry to the group on what look like false terms are lambasted as undermining someone else's fundamental truth. In the

81

context of communities historically marginalised because of their race or nationality, this is often described as 'cultural appropriation': the act of trying on superficial elements of a culture without appreciating their essence – in particular, the elements that have historically caused people of that culture to be overlooked or actively oppressed. It is no more than an approximation of what Hall describes as 'the common historical experiences and shared cultural codes'[6] that constitute cultural identity. In 2019, the singer Adele's Instagram featured a photo of her dressed up to go to Notting Hill carnival – a celebration of Caribbean culture in west London – wearing a Jamaican flag bikini and with Bantu knots in her hair. She was widely criticised for appropriating black culture to look good.

Cultural appropriation is offensive and perpetuates oppression because it is a form of colonisation – stealing something from people with less power and removing its cultural significance. It also perpetuates stereotypes, reducing a culture to its most obvious markers and taking them out of context. But if its crime is inauthenticity, cultural appropriation depends on there being an authentic culture to appropriate in the first place. In a 2019 op-ed for the *Guardian*, the writer and activist Ash Sarkar challenged this:

> When you're a second- or third-generation migrant, your ties to your heritage can feel a little precarious. You're a foreigner here, you're a tourist back in your ancestral land, and home is the magpie nest you construct of the bits of culture you're able to hold close. The appropriation

debate peddles a comforting lie that there's such thing as a stable and authentic connection to culture that can remain intact after the seismic interruptions of colonialism and migration.[7]

A stable and authentic connection to culture in any context can also appear to provide a stable and authentic connection to the self – and so in a society equally obsessed with individual authenticity, the attraction of a definitive, authentic *group* identity is stronger than ever. However, for any feelings of uncertainty about the individual self to be assuaged, the common identity must maintain its stability. In *What White People Can Do Next*, Emma Dabiri argues that fixed identity categories – here in the context of race – are not necessarily empowering of the marginalised group but the oppressing group, because repeatedly acknowledging your identity as an oppressor perpetuates the idea that it's true, fixing it as inevitable and simultaneously excusing you from participating in activism.[8] 'The more you state and claim your "whiteness", without doing any further work to unpack what that means,' she writes, 'the more you become fixed to that articulation of self, the more you become wedded to whiteness.'[9] In other words, the more 'whiteness' and 'blackness' are legitimised as essential, concrete categories, the more those categories entrench the divisions that they are ostensibly supposed to bridge. Whiteness is, Dabiri argues, necessarily bound up in notions of superiority.[10] Claiming it as an identity may be a good-faith attempt to acknowledge one's 'privilege', but it also allows that privilege to become part of the unimpeachable authentic self. 'If somebody else's inferiority is a necessary prerequisite for your own sense of self,' she writes, 'you are somewhat trapped, if not doomed.'[11]

Egregious attempts by individuals to distance themselves from their social group can be equally jarring. When the model Emily Ratajkowski complains in her book of essays *My Body* about the 'rich people' she observes while sitting on the beach on a free holiday to the Maldives,[12] or when former public schoolboys dress head-to-toe in shabby vintage sportswear and speak in urban slang, the sense of defensiveness about what they clearly know to be part of their identity simply affirms its presence.

More broadly, attaching the individual self to a fixed definition of a group self – and the group definition subsequently becoming entrenched – can lead to polarisation and even extremism. If you depend on a solid group identity to find individual stability, any questioning of that group also causes individual agony; identity is deeply emotional. And so, if a group's identity is challenged – as British national identity has been, for example, in the past few decades of increased immigration and globalisation – it fragments into the new version and a more stubbornly held iteration of the old, which enables the individuals within the group to maintain their own senses of self. It follows that each old version becomes increasingly extreme or more concentrated. That is not just because it is smaller, but because the individuals within it pour in the same emotional significance they once did to the larger group: a narrower definition of the collective self is given the same weight.

The fragmenting of a shared 'one true self' naturally dismantles the idea that the original group ever possessed fixed attributes. There is not one true collective self but two or more, which undermines the position of truth – an idea that has played out in the 'gender wars' fought by the British media over the question of what defines a woman. Again, we witness that, where authenticity is paramount, two versions of the truth cannot exist simultaneously. In *The Divided Self*, a study of schizophrenia based on the premise of the constructed 'false self', the psychoanalyst RD Laing writes:

> It seems… that the preferred method of attack on the other is based on the same principle as the attack felt to be implicit in the other's relationship to oneself. Thus, the man who is frightened of his own subjectivity being swamped, impinged upon, or congealed by the other is frequently to be found attempting to swamp, to impinge upon, or to kill the other person's subjectivity.[13]

More often than not, culture wars are started when who *you* are appears to challenge someone else's sense of who *they* are.

*

This process has played out clearly in the case of British nationalism, notably in the run-up to and aftermath of the 2016 Brexit referendum. Some saw Britain's membership of the EU as strengthening nationhood by binding the country to a broader group with a more diverse and fluid sense of identity. An alternative view is that the EU corrupted the purity of British identity. The Vote Leave campaign was based on ideas about autonomy – exemplified by the slogan 'take back control' – and authenticity, whereby independence from the bloc would enable a more cohesive, unified, self-determining nation to emerge. A key determining factor of Remain and Leave voters was education – of voters under 34, 80 per cent of those with a degree voted to remain compared to 37 per cent without.[14] Higher education has been shown to have a positive correlation with liberal values and the prioritisation of individual rights. In contrast, people who didn't go to college or university are shown generally to attribute more importance to hierarchy, tradition and a stable sense of group identity.[15]

Of course, this essential 'Britishness' was largely defined by immigration, or the preferred lack of it. 72 per cent of those who voted to leave felt that immigration had 'undermined British culture'[16] – a phenomenon that naturally affects the individual sense of self if that sense of self is bound up with Britishness. And so if you are attempting to use nationality to define who you are as, for example, a white person brought up in what you perceive to be a traditionally 'British' way (which might include Christian values, working in a major British industry, or partaking in something as seemingly trivial as pub culture), but the nation in front of you doesn't look white or Christian and doesn't engage in the traditions you do, your own inner sense of authenticity could be threatened. You cannot be who you are – British – unless Britain looks like you.

When this threat to meaning occurs, and the prized inner self is confused with some outer manifestation of identity, we witness attempts to change or protect the preferred sense of group identity in order to protect the self. In 2020, when the murder of George Floyd by a police officer in Minneapolis triggered a surge of Black Lives Matter (BLM) and anti-racism protests worldwide, questions of cultural identity were raised in respect of history. At a BLM protest in Bristol, protestors toppled a life-size bronze statue of the slave-trader Edward Colston (which for many years local groups had campaigned to remove) and threw it in the nearby harbour. This led to weeks of impassioned debate in the UK about problematic figures being idolised in monuments, and the so-called 'erasure' of history involved in removing them – a conversation that, the historian David Olusoga argued in the *Guardian*, caused the real anti-racism movement to be 'blown off course'.[17] This derailing was to the advantage of those in power, who did not particularly want to address the issues that the protests brought to public attention such as police violence, health inequality and a lack of black representation in powerful institutions.

What Olusoga calls the 'Statue Wars'[18] were not primarily, or at least directly, about racism. They were about identity. Most anti-racist activists would agree that any aggrandisement in bronze of problematic historical figures is 'a symptom of the problem, not the problem itself'.[19] At the time, it was widely accepted that those most passionate about monuments were not the BLM protestors, who were busy trying to effect systemic equality, but those who saw the removal of Colston and others as a threat to their own identity. The removal or displacement of historical artefacts that are literally set in stone leads to a metaphorical instability of other previously solid-seeming facets of identity. In the weeks following the original BLM protests and Colston's toppling, counter-protests were organised by far-right organisations such as Britain First and the Democratic Football Lads' Alliance. Hundreds of people travelled to London to 'defend memorials' and 'protect' statues such as that of Winston Churchill in Parliament Square, which had been defaced with graffiti reading '[Winston Churchill] was a racist'. One group of protestors was widely mocked online for ring-fencing the statue of George Eliot, who actively opposed slavery, in the Warwickshire town of Nuneaton. One of the protestors told the *Daily Mail*: 'I'm here purely to protect our history'.[20] In reality, it is hard not to infer that he was trying to protect his sense of self.

*

Feminism, particularly in the UK, is also plagued by fear of 'subjectivity being swamped, impinged upon, or congealed by the other'[21] and is torn by the question of authentic womanhood. Gender identity theory, popularised by the philosopher Judith Butler in the late 1980s, suggested that gender was not irrevocably bound up with your biological sex but was an innate feeling that could then be realised in the world via performance.[22] Transgender people, of course, existed long before Butler, but the reach of gender identity theory changed perceptions of what it meant to be trans. Where before being trans meant something material – that you had changed your sex or performed gender with hormones, surgery or clothing – now it meant something intrinsic: that your inner sense of your gender did not match the gender you were 'assigned at birth' based on your sex.

Gender studies is infinitely more complex than a crude distinction between our inner and outer selves, but the broader language of authenticity pervades much writing on gender identity. The LGBTQ charity Stonewall defines gender identity as 'A person's innate sense of their own gender, whether male, female or something else';[23] in the Yogyakarta Principles, a document on human rights about gender and sexuality written in 2006 at a meeting of inter-national human rights groups, it is asserted that 'No one shall be subjected to pressure to conceal, suppress or deny' their gender identity.[24] The notable increase in diagnoses of gender dysphoria (a disconnect between your gender identity and the gender you were assigned at birth according to your sex) and subsequent increase in the number of referrals to gender identity clinics in the last decade is often described in conservative media as a dangerous 'trend' led by woke snowflakes whose only agenda is to have their own feelings validated. This is a vicious culture war fuelled by prejudice and fear of the other – and it often manifests in direct criticism of the espousal of authenticity and truth-living at all costs.

Yet those who oppose the inclusion of trans people as part of their gender identity group are just as beholden to the principles of authenticity, and so any such argument – even aside from the fact that it contributes to the active oppression of a tiny minority of people who are often already vulnerable – has little weight. An essentialist definition of gender that corresponds exactly with biological sex may not appear so preoccupied with being authentically yourself but is preoccupied with whether or not you are an authentic man or woman. The most heated protestations against defining trans women as women and trans men as men stem from the alleged or potential *inauthenticity* of the individual in question. There is an anxiety that people could exploit a more fluid group definition and therefore get away with disguising who they really are – for example, that a predatory cisgender man will pretend to be trans so he can gain access to women's spaces and harm women, or that a male sportsperson would deliberately participate in women's sport on the grounds of gender identity in order to win. The debate in sport has extended beyond trans people to athletes such as Caster Semenya, an intersex woman with naturally elevated levels of testosterone, who has appealed the rules set by World Athletics in 2019, which specified that women such as Semenya must suppress their testosterone levels to participate in women's events. Here we can see that even outside the gender identity debate, the group cannot be neatly defined by biology alone.

As well as a general unease about perceived inauthenticity, trans-exclusionary radical feminists (often known by the much-contested term 'TERFs') and 'gender-critical' feminists (and others who believe transgender women should not be allowed in the same identity category as cisgender women) are often concerned with the idea that the oppression of women has historically been based on matters of biology and physicality: male aggression, the trauma of childbirth, sexual assault, having medical problems ignored. The idea that anyone who does not have first-hand experience of those phenomena, or fully understand the threat of them, could attempt to be part of the same category is offensive to some cisgender women – and, seemingly inexplicably, plenty of cis-gender men – who view transness as a kind of appropriation, a cosplay of their historic struggle. (Of course, this negates the fact that trans people, by diverting from the patriarchal norm, also have to contend with male aggression, assault and being sidelined in medical settings.) In other words, there is a fixed, substantive definition of womanhood that can only be met by having certain characteristics. That this definition includes, or has historically resulted in, oppression explains why the question of whether trans women are women dominates much more of the public discourse than whether trans men are men.

If all gender is performance, there is arguably nothing substantial to appropriate. Of Simone de Beauvoir's well-known assertion in *The Second Sex* that 'one is not born a woman, but, rather, becomes one',[25] Butler writes in *Gender Trouble*: 'There is nothing in her account that guarantees the 'one' who becomes a woman is necessarily female'.[26] Conversely, the philosophy professor Kathleen Stock – who in 2021 resigned from her post at the University of Sussex after students hounded her for her gender-critical views – emphasises the well-trodden but important argument that

91

'womanhood' is also itself an oppressive framework, and challenges the idea that a woman is something you would want to 'become'. 'When some twentieth-century feminists talked in de Beauvoir-esque vein about "becoming a woman",' she writes in *Material Girls*, 'they meant having a set of social norms or expectations about femininity imposed upon you, not having an "inner" identity of a certain kind.'[27]

Here Stock exposes one of the most egregious stumbling blocks of the gender-critical movement: feminism is *precisely* about 'having an "inner" identity of a certain kind'. Stock writes that 'feminists wanted to escape the historically persistent idea that a woman's personality, behaviour and life options are determined by her female biology, making her naturally suited for home life rather than professional work or intellectual life'[28] – because, we understand, professional work or intellectual life may have better reflected her authentic interests. Whether de Beauvoir meant that 'becoming a woman' involved constructing the self via performance or being forced into a stereotype because of society's reading of your identity, twentieth-century feminism was focused on liberating women from whatever box they found themselves in. It allowed them to be their authentic selves, not simply be tarnished with the label 'woman' and all its historic connotations. And so, perhaps the woman's body is not her definitive identity marker but the final frontier of oppression; transness, in escaping the social boundaries that your body imposes on you, is arguably the ultimate liberation.

Feminism, then, is about the freedom to construct an authentic self and not to be judged by your external identity markers, regardless of the body you were born in. Nothing in this idea precludes trans women from being women, or indeed trans men from being men. Yet because the female body has historically been the subject of violence and individual selves have been constructed around an identity defined in those terms (perhaps because those individuals have been the subjects of violence, too), some cisgender women seek to maintain the boundaries of gender that have historically defined their authentic experience as individuals. Questioning the parameters of their identity as women has caused their understanding of themselves to rupture; if womanhood requires authenticity, there can only be one version of it. And this is why we witness some people not only ring-fencing their own metaphorical statue but vandalising someone else's, invalidating trans people's existence entirely. People are found, in other words, 'attempting to swamp, to impinge upon, or to kill the other person's subjectivity'.[29]

*

If identity groups are defined by strict boundaries, they naturally jar with the idea of a wholly free inner self. Yet the question of individual authenticity – or perhaps the *right* to individual authenticity – has always been at the heart of identity politics, as Davies and Fukuyama recognise. The term 'identity politics' originates from the Combahee River Collective, a 1970s group of black, lesbian, feminist socialists who felt disillusioned with other black liberation movements and white-dominated women's movements that did not fully recognise their experience. In a statement issued in 1977, they wrote a manifesto for 'Black Feminism' explaining why their specific identity justifies a politics of its own, hinting at the importance of intersectionality. 'We… find it difficult to separate race from class from sex oppression because in our lives they are most often experienced simultaneously,' they wrote. 'We know that there is such a thing as racial-sexual oppression which is neither solely racial nor solely sexual.'[30] The ultimate aim was to be liberated from this oppression, ultimately to be able to express the authentic self. 'Our politics initially sprang from the shared belief that Black women are inherently valuable, that our liberation is a necessity not as an adjunct to somebody else's but because of our need as human persons for autonomy… We reject pedestals, queenhood, and walking ten paces behind. To be recognized as human, levelly human, is enough.'[31]

To be recognised as 'levelly human' is, arguably, the central struggle for marginalised groups. Identity politics is not necessarily about realising your inner self as a result of your identity, but in spite of it. 'The broadening and universalisation of dignity turns the private quest for self into a political project,' writes Fukuyama:[32] dignity that comes from being recognised on a deeper level than simply your perceptible identity, and which therefore implicitly recognises people of that identity as equally important, and as worthy of rights, as others. Individuality within the group is crucial to allow for fluidity.

In this sense, the search for pure authenticity requires a certain level of privilege. A rambling, all-encompassing quest for authenticity of self can only be embarked on if somebody has the freedom to make certain choices. In fact, the more overwhelming the choice, the more difficult authenticity can be to find. It is those with more limited options for whom authenticity of self may not historically have been possible, and for whom being recognised as a human being with feelings and a unique personality becomes a radical proposition. And while authenticity involves overcoming one's circumstances to 'live your truth', identity nudges us towards acceptance. The circumstances that have built you – if you are of a certain race, nationality, appearance, disability, etc. – can be embraced, not escaped or suppressed. In a world where living your truth has become synonymous, in some cases, with a particular type of lifestyle, it is important to acknowledge that that 'truth' looks different for everyone.

*

With this in mind, a culture of accepting and then performing 'who we are' leads to an exaggeration of more trivial identity tropes. As historic group identities like nation, race and gender become less stable, we naturally look for other fixed sets of characteristics to which to bind ourselves. The excessive taxonomisation of every micro-trend that occurs online – which often involves adding the suffix 'core' to any given word – is exhausting evidence of our desire to belong to a group, or perhaps our inability to let things be fluid and changing. Unlike countercultures such as punk or even emo, contemporary aesthetic trends like 'cottagecore' and 'indie sleaze' exist primarily online and represent little beyond their own frame of image references or nostalgia. Still, they offer something reassuringly definitive to which to attach ourselves when traditional frames of reference for identity are in question, and the pressure to be who we are feels inescapable. We want to put margins around everything and be able to come down on one side of any given argument. Online we can convey that we are a specific type of person and create tribes based purely on image – which are also easily identifiable by others.

The astrology trend of the mid-2010s and beyond exemplifies a seemingly trivial yet powerful manifestation of identity. Far from the fortune-cookie wisdom of 1980s newspaper horoscopes, contemporary astrology is a complex web, the deep understanding of which yields an image of the authentic self – but an authentic self necessarily defined by the identities of each 'sign'. Many people who read their horoscope or analyse their birth chart know they don't believe in it. Still, it is appealing because of its certainty in its predictions of the future and clearly defined categories in the present – both of which function on confirmation bias. Looking through the list of star signs, I could probably identify with the traits of any one of them, but that I *am* a Capricorn means that I nod along easily to the somewhat questionable ideas that I am practical and financially ruthless than, say, the extroversion that I might notice in myself had I been born in August.

Astrology – like other pseudo-scientific methods of deducing your personality such as the Enneagram, or even the countless quizzes on *Buzzfeed* that offer to align your personality with the essence of pretty much any object in the world – also professes to encompass the complexities of the human condition using impenetrably vague and yet highly specialised detail. In astrology, each planet corresponds with a particular facet of life (this is why you shouldn't buy washing machines during Mercury retrograde). This means that each area of your life is influenced by the sign its corresponding planet was in when you were born, and any disconnect with what you think is your star sign – your 'sun sign' – can be eliminated by simply probing deeper into your chart (I may be a Capricorn, but I also have people-pleasing tendencies; luckily, these are explained by my Libra rising). Within the astrology ecosystem, there is an explanation for virtually every element of self: the more precise these systems are, the more they assimilate something like 'authenticity'.

The internet has made it easier to define specific group identities, and also for people to find groups with whom they identify. Of course, this process is part of the extensive choice offered by pursuing authenticity – not just some organic process of realisation but the opportunity to 'find your people' and to see your inner self reflected in someone else. In some cases, this lends itself, again, to dangerous extremism. Identification with a group can justify feelings of anger and disillusionment that feel very much part of the inner self but are, in fact, a result of the circumstances of one's life. The 'involuntary celibate' (incel) community – a group of (mostly) men who define themselves by believing that others deem them too repulsive for sex – epitomises this process. They turn their hatred outwards onto the world of promiscuous 'Chads and Stacys' who don't have the problems they have – resulting, sometimes, in murder. Elliot Rodger killed six people in an attack in California in 2014, aged 22. Before the murders, he declared in a YouTube video that he had 'no choice but to exact revenge on the society' that had 'denied' him sex. The incel community subsequently idolised Rodger as 'The Supreme Gentleman'. He was 'hailed' on Facebook by Alek Minassian in 2018, minutes before he murdered ten people in the name of an 'incel rebellion'.

Incel culture and ideology show an extreme version of the inner self becoming embedded in a constructed identity – here, of course, one in which misogyny is intrinsic. Incels actively render their celibacy inevitable by counting themselves as members of the community; their continued separation from society is a self-fulfilling prophecy that keeps the group identity stable. Its 'authenticity' is boosted by the idea that incels have woken up to the realities of the world – 'taken the red pill', to return to *The Matrix*. Though many men who call themselves incels are young and could simply have waited longer for sex or a relationship, they choose instead to reject the prospect and ensure their assumed identity, as someone who does not have relationships, is combined with their sense of self. They are self-professedly not 'levelly human' with 'Chads and Stacys'. Sometimes this constructed lack of dignity manifests in hatred of women, describing them as 'femoids' who are 'subhuman', but sometimes accusations of 'subhumanness' are levelled at themselves. On incel forums online, self-hatred abounds due to what is perceived as an unchangeable difference between them and everyone else. A stubbornly held certainty of the authentic individual identity becomes political: *It is not me that should change,* they think, *but society.*[33]

*

Contempt for inauthenticity unites the two sides of any given culture war. Nothing could be worse, for either side, than the cardinal sin of virtue-signalling – empty gestures towards progressivism that do little more than further the agenda of the brand, personal or corporate. The National Trust began to give more attention to the scope of the information available in their exhibitions after the Black Lives Matter protests in 2020 and was faced with outcry by those who see it as a beloved British institution that should know better than to descend into performative wokeism. Though the National Trust's campaign was not simply a panicked reaction to the protests – they had begun work on it months previously – other virtue-signalling behaviours were rife in the aftermath of the BLM 2020 movement, such as the 'Blackout Tuesday' campaign in which social media users went silent for a day, posting nothing but a black square on Instagram in solidarity with black people, and then promptly moved on with their lives.

Social media has tipped us further into the divisive essentialism of identity politics, which demands that we conform to a type, take a position, and move through a process of binary decisions until we have reached a destination easily identifiable to 'outsiders'. Of course, curating our various selves on social media is also a process of creating an easily identifiable type. There's only so much we can convey, and even the extent to which we reveal ourselves gives away something about us. Social media naturally creates tribes as we copy each other and attempt to convey who we are to the world.

Living out the collective authenticity of a group is a way to overthrow societal structures. Sexuality, for example, can be deliberately hidden and suppressed (less easily than the more externally obvious attributes of, say, ethnicity or gender), so it is by definition authentic when it outs: something from the inside has surfaced. Identity and authenticity are not diametrically opposed as outer and inner selves; as 'society's perception of me' and the 'real, inner me'. Authenticity is also crucial to identity as a collective property – a quality that enables you to belong to a certain group, which should, in turn, give you a sense of community or perhaps a role in the world that assuages the identity crisis. It cannot be true that the circumstances that have unfolded in your life have no bearing whatsoever on 'who you are'. But they are not the sum total of who you are, either.

In his book *The Lies That Bind*, Kwame Anthony Appiah writes that modes of identity can 'become forms of confinement… But they can also give contours to our freedom.'[34] A more fluid approach to identity is possible without the ropes of authenticity. Perhaps who you are is fixed, but your definitive qualities are not. Perhaps you are not defined by the fixed identity of the group to which you belong; rather, the group to which you belong is able to change its qualities based on the fluidity of the individuals within it. These knots are tightly tied, but – in order to speak productively about identity; to redraw the line between empathy and selfishness; and, most importantly, to protect people whose freedoms are limited – we must begin to disentangle them.

PURITY

Our authenticity obsession is not just about being ourselves –
it's about becoming them. A narrative notion of authenticity
can be found in Nietzsche's autobiography *Ecce Homo* (sub-
titled, in some translations, 'How To Become What You
Are'), in the pop psychology obsession with 'journeys', and
in the very first scene of Lena Dunham's *Girls* ('I have work,'
says Hannah, 'and then I have a dinner thing, and then I am
busy, trying to become who I am.').[1] Becoming who we are
when we are under so much cultural pressure to do so can
feel all-consuming and exhausting. We are surrounded by
products that profess to help us and encumbered by decisions that could change our path forever. We have to make
decisions, too, not just about who to be but about what
methods we should use to realise ourselves. On Nietzsche's
reading, there are 'no standards that determine whether one
is doing a proper job of self-making', as Charles Guignon
puts it in *On Being Authentic*.[2] But in contemporary culture, it

feels like we are under pressure to get it right. Perhaps partly as a distraction from the task's impossibility, we become just as fixated on the idea of the journey. Ignoring even that authenticity is an abstract aim, the question remains: how do we get there?

Historically, religion has provided answers. Faith not only gives us a moral code by which to live but attaches our sense of being to something larger, something with purpose; Augustine wrote in the fourth century that the way to stabilise the self was to bind it to God.[3] The practice of religion has significantly declined – in the 2011 census, 25 per cent of people in the UK said they had no religion compared to 15 per cent in 2001. A YouGov survey in December 2020 found that almost half of those in the UK who now identify as Christian (still the dominant faith by far) do not consider their religion an important part of their life.[4] The quest for the true self – the best self – and the subsequent worship of performances of self on social media has taken over as the predominant spiritual undertaking of our time.

In many ways, this is freeing. Beyond the platitudinous – go with your gut, follow your heart, know yourself – there is no prescribed moral code. But the lack of a code leaves society bereft. Combined with capitalism's competitive, individualist atmosphere, the spiritual mandate for authenticity has yielded a world in which individuals float in a sea of infinite choice, lost and anxious, desperately trying to find an anchor. This might come, or not come, in the form of identity groups; the comforting certainty of social media, where we can watch our true selves blossom before our very eyes; or a product that yields a moment of truthfulness in its temporary thrill.

Guignon writes that on a Romantic view of authenticity, 'self-discovery is not a matter of finding an entity that has been there all along. It is a matter of making the self in the course of the search.'[5] As we continue to make ourselves in our devotional practice of authenticity, pathways are forming – tried and tested methods to realise the inner self. In their mutual prescriptiveness, these methods compete to be the best way to create a life of incorruptible truth, and in their opposition to one another – with the logical conclusion that both versions of 'truth' cannot exist – they expose that authenticity is often a hollow goal.

*

Phillip McGraw, *Oprah*'s Dr Phil, summarised the modern conception of authenticity in his 2001 bestseller *Self Matters: Creating Your Life from the Inside Out*. He asked 'what you might choose for your self if… you hadn't inherited the status quo; if you weren't born into a certain family and station in life and weren't buried so deep that you seemed to have no choices'.[6] There is 'a whole other level of existence, distinct from what you do, that is the real, true, genuine sum and substance of who you are'.[7] 'The authentic self,' he wrote, 'is the *you* that can be found at your absolute core… It is all of your strengths and values that are uniquely yours and need expression.'[8] In other words, the authentic self is buried deep within and must be uncovered for you to be free.

That this is still the widely held belief today means that authenticity-seeking pursuits often involve a kind of stripping back, a shedding of layers. This is an exclusionary approach to authenticity: ruling out what you are *not* to become more clearly what you *are*. It is a whittling down to the essential self buried within. By peeling back layers of circumstance and external influence, you can become the quintessential version of yourself. This connotes a kind of minimalism – which as a genre of design and art is influenced by Zen, the Buddhist spiritual practice that originated in Japan. In Buddhism, the individual self is an illusion; in Zen, the path to enlightenment is through adopting a 'middle way' between self and no-self. Meanwhile, minimalism's approximations in the West look sleek and effortless and often have self at the centre – it's all 'who I am', without much 'trying' or 'becoming'.

As minimalism exploded in the mid-2010s as a fashion and design trend, I was briefly swept up in its allure. In 2016, two years after I met someone who had thrown away all but four items of clothing, I visited a friend, peeked into her housemate's room and saw calm and order. It was not just tidy, but a space in which there could not have been any mess. There was a sparsely populated clothes rail, a bare floor, a plant, and very little else. I found out that this was not necessarily her natural state of being and rather a con- trived effort to change her life after I remarked to my friend that the housemate also seemed to have thrown away her bed – something I, a maximalist, deemed to be a relatively essential item – and opted instead for a mattress on the floor. Next to the mattress were a couple of books, stacked, with a lamp on top. Needless to say, it made me want to rip up my life and start all over again.

Later that year, like so many others, I began a self-purification process myself and bought Marie Kondo's best-selling book *The Life-Changing Magic of Tidying*. I wasn't going to start sleeping on a mattress on the floor, but I did want what the book promised me: a reflection in what I owned of who I really was. All I had to do was pick up each of my possessions in turn, ask myself if it 'sparks joy',[9] and then either give it to a charity shop or watch a YouTube video about how to fold it. I could almost taste the impending clarity. The metaphor was embarrassingly obvious: I wanted my big messy life and chaotic mind neatly compartmentalised into metaphorical stackable Muji boxes. Still, Kondo's adages were undeniably reassuring. Visualise the life you want. Listen to your inner voice. Put your house in order, and then your life can truly begin.

Implicit in Kondo's instructions is the idea that the self brought into being by this purification process already exists – it's just obscured by all the stuff on the floor. And so its appeal is mainly in its simplicity. The work of becoming yourself is relieved by following Kondo's rules: all you have to do is *be* yourself, tapping into a feeling of authenticity to discern what sparks joy, and you will be left with a perfect image of yourself to behold and understand. The hope is that 'tidying up' will realise the self in the material world and allow the duality of you, the physical being, and yourself, the inner being, to exist in perfect harmony. 'What a concord is proposed – between me and my own self,' as Trilling wrote in

Sincerity and Authenticity: 'Were ever two beings better suited to each other?'[10]

The mass purging of possessions brought on by the Marie Kondo craze and other tidying 'hacks' popular with YouTubers, such as the beautifully clickable 'Swedish death cleaning', has since broadened into something more holistic. The cultural edict for cleanliness of self may not be expressed in such terms, but the injunction to avoid its opposite, 'toxicity', is everywhere. 'Is your relationship toxic?' we are asked. 'Is your attitude to work toxic? Your friendships? Your eating habits? Are you suffering from toxic positivity?' In July 2022 the women's magazine *Stylist* ran an article helpfully outlining the '6 signs you're in a toxic relationship with yourself – and what you can do about it'.[11] The connotations of the word are serious: polluted, corrupted, poisonous. 'Dump him!!!!' is the cry of well-intentioned social media users hoping to guide a woman back to her true path. We are called upon, urgently, to banish anything 'toxic' from our lives to cut back to something pure and sanctified, something authentic.

Purging your life of possessions, people and behaviours that, as the saying goes, 'no longer serve you' (as though the 'service' of individuals is the point of not only possessions but people and behaviours) is appealing because it appears to get you a little closer to that quintessential self at your absolute core. We are led to believe – frequently by the brands responsible for it – that our lives are cluttered and overwhelming, that we need 'hacks' to help us do basic tasks and stop feeling so bad. If we eliminate all that clutter, we will be left with the serene self that lives within us, able to cruise through life feeling calm and happy.

The idea of capitalist overwhelm also allows us to relinquish responsibility for how we feel and behave. It seems many people fail to appreciate that becoming your purest self is precisely one of the values that create such pressure – and that shifting the blame onto everything less pure than yourself, be it 'toxic' relationships or 'burnout' culture, perpetuates the idea that all we can rely on is the individual. When millennials say they don't know 'how to adult', for example, there is no suggestion that it could be their own fault and that they should simply learn how to read their electricity meter. It is a way of sanctifying the individual at odds with the systems that appear to have prevented it from reaching its full potential.

The draw of this type of thinking, where the self is an untouchable, fixed entity, is that it is fundamentally optimistic. The 'true' self is unquestioningly equated with the best self. The assumption is that whatever we find underneath the layers of toxicity or clutter will be better than the self we were before; similarly, if we presume that we already contain the 'best version' of ourselves, we can begin to think we are, in fact, better than we are. Once you start to believe that you already have the components of a super-you inside yourself, and all you have to do is discover them, it will become much easier to overcome whatever hurdles you have identified as holding you back until now. Then, if you succeed in making yourself the best you can be, you are creating a wholly pure kind of authenticity.

*

Wellness – an amalgamation of the mellow vibes of the New Age and the uptight narcissism of social media – is, perhaps counterintuitively, a natural product of authenticity culture. It is the starkest manifestation of the exclusionary approach to becoming ourselves, in which the best self and the true self are one and the same – and a state that can be achieved, as the *Atlantic* journalist Amanda Mull wrote in 2019, by 'buying things until you feel better'.[12] Most of all, wellness is an exercise in realising potential.

Here, purifying the body is considered essential to becoming the best and most true version of yourself. A physical version of eliminating 'toxicity', it is emblematic of dedication to purity in the exclusionary approach. Using the body, the physical manifestation of self, to nurture and shape the inner self encourages the idea that the self is one contained whole. If the outer self or the obstacles to the true self can be reduced mainly to lifestyle choices such as diet, exercise and 'morning routines', the path to finding the self is clear and straightforward. Wellness invites curiosity and certainty simultaneously. You do not know who or what the self is that you're aiming for – you are simply (to use a bit of wellness vernacular) trusting the process – and yet you are also employing a strict rigidity in the choices and sacrifices you must make to become 'well'.

Similarly, wellness embodies a tension between a genuine attempt to find meaning and a somewhat naive trust in consumerism. Wellness culture lost much of its mainstream appeal in the latter half of the 2010s because it began to feel less like inner peace and more like worrying about smoothie bowls; less like going against the grain and more like going with it; less like a miracle and more like a scam. Gwyneth Paltrow's wellness brand, Goop, was subjected to a $145,000 fine in 2018 for its 'unsubstantiated' claims about solid-jade eggs designed for vaginal insertion. Goop said the eggs (which cost $66 each and come with a handy storage bag) 'balance hormones, regulate menstrual cycles, prevent uterine prolapse, and increase bladder control'.[13] A court ruled that Goop not only had to pay the fine and reimburse customers who had bought the products but that they could not make any future claims about the efficacy of their products without reliable scientific evidence. More outrageously, in 2017 the Australian Instagrammer Belle Gibson was fined £240,000 by the Australian government after she had claimed clean eating had cured her terminal brain cancer. A lymphoma patient named Kylie, who in 2013 was six months into chemotherapy treatment, told the BBC in 2021 that she was drawn to Gibson's methods and subsequently gave up the chemo in favour of Gibson's diet because she was 'dying on the inside, getting worse with every single treatment' while Gibson was 'out there living her best life'.[14] Gibson, it turned out, never had cancer in the first place.

The central tenets of wellness culture – purification, spirituality, physical optimisation, capitalism and, of course, authenticity – come together in luxury spinning classes. Popularised by the New York studio Soul Cycle in the late 2000s, this type of indoor cycling is intense cardiovascular exercise but also a ritualised primal frenzy that leaves you feeling emotionally and physically cleansed. The continued popularity of these classes in fast-paced, expensive cities is not just because they help you achieve the ideal athletic body. They offer something more: an almost cultish sense of community and the promise of connecting with the self.

This is designed to be a spiritual experience as much as a physical one. As you ride to the beat of the deafening music, the instructor intones various life-affirming stock phrases such as 'let something go', 'ask yourself what brought you here today', and 'for forty-five minutes, it's just about you'. Pedalling furiously, you begin to believe that you can be better, feel better, be true to yourself.

Positivity is, again, part of the process here. Unlike other forms of cultish, high-intensity exercise such as CrossFit, spiritual spinning rarely involves pushing yourself to extreme discomfort. Instead, progress is encouraged by a sort of confirmation bias. We are told we are already good enough – the person we want to be is already inside us – and we should only exercise within the scope of our authentic limits. When the instructor does invite you to increase the intensity, it is rarely at the expense of who you are (somebody, perhaps, who really doesn't want to increase the intensity). In the 'blackout track', when all the lights are turned off, and the class is invited to freestyle, you are told to listen to your inner voice to tell you what your body needs. Nobody can see you: there is, theoretically, no fear of judgement, which invites freedom to follow your authentic instinct to rest or work. The blackout track also instils in participants just enough agency to feel reassured that however they feel when they leave the class is a result of their own authentic choice. They have become, in other words, a little bit more themselves.

It hardly needs saying that such an experience is expensive – attendance in London costs around £25 a class. The exclusivity of luxury spinning is part of its appeal – you get a fluffy towel and free conditioner to complement your spiritual awakening. It also ensures that the business of clean, clear purity of self is reserved for people with money. This is mirrored across wellness culture and made all the more egregious because it creates a vicious cycle: the result is a positive correlation between people who present as more authentically in tune with themselves and those who present as moneyed. Rich and self-realised – in direct contradiction to the notion of authenticity as anything gritty and flawed – become synonymous.

It is this shiny, wealthy image that has ultimately been wellness's downfall. The exclusionary approach to authenticity, which is appealing for the simple, mess-free life that it offers, is in fact exclusionary in more than one sense. How could something with the aim of purifying the self be so corrupt, so elitist, such a scam? Could there be another way?

*

As the elite methods of the exclusionary approach became exhausting towards the end of the 2010s, a different path seemed to appear – one of inclusion. There was no need to be able to afford boutique exercise studios, change your diet or cultivate a capsule wardrobe to become yourself. Instead, a new approach encouraged acceptance and impulsivity. In the exclusionary approach, we reduce, hone and perfect; in the inclusionary approach, we grow, accumulate and accept. While in the exclusionary approach we find the true self by eradicating what we are not, in the inclusionary approach we build the self by adding on things that we are. In the exclusionary approach, we tidy up – in the inclusionary approach, we make a mess.

The inclusionary approach represents an alternative way of viewing the self: not as a fixed thing to be uncovered, but as something to be built or accumulated. The inclusive approach embraces chaos and yields an authentic self via a total lack of repression or resistance – by accepting what happens to you. There is a sense of gradually giving way to the true self via the process of living rather than reaching an ultimate authenticity. While the exclusionary approach strips back layers of societal conditioning to reveal the self contained within, the inclusive, all-encompassing approach invites that self to burst forth actively, either overriding any external influences or simply embracing them as part of the authentic whole.

At this end of the spectrum, chaos is fetishised. On social media, this can manifest in a kind of 'anti-aesthetic' aesthetic. In February 2022, Daisy Jones wrote for *Vice* that Instagram had evolved from pictures of 'a plush hotel room… or some perfectly shot latte art next to an open book' (the exclusionary approach) to 'a random car number plate, a flash-on pic of some fast food and… a dead pigeon squashed in the road'[15] (the inclusionary approach). The enjoyment of, or respect for, mess is a pushback against the inauthenticity of the optimisation obsession that came before. The inclusionary, all-encompassing approach to authenticity in the internet age demonstrates a dogged dedication to accepting – and documenting – what *is*, rather than striving for betterment. In January 2022 an anti-New Year's resolutions article in the *Guardian* suggested that 'By being intelligently, purposely lazier; less mindful, disorganised, slower (and with a bit of self-compassion), we might actually be more successful, productive and happier, but' – and this bit is crucial – 'on our own terms'.[16]

This may appear to be a less paradoxical approach to authenticity than the exclusionary method, but there are still contradictions within it. A commitment to messiness carries a different kind of inflexibility – a stubbornness, reminiscent of the hipster's, against the status quo. The inclusionary approach also risks a loss of agency because you have to include within the scope of the self influences that would, from an exclusionary perspective, have the potential to contaminate your true essence. The inclusionary approach gives into impulses whose provenance is unknown: they could originate from the depths of the soul or from some sponsored content you scrolled past the other day. Who knows, and who cares? By embracing the full spectrum of influence, you implant yourself firmly in the real world.

In the phenomenon of 'self-care' these contradictions are clear – as are the reasons this route to authenticity is so attractive. The origins of the phrase have been hashed out extensively online since it became a hot topic in the mid-2010s: it was popularised during the civil rights and women's movements when it became clear that systemic problems in the medical system were preventing doctors from tending to the needs of marginalised groups. Self-care represented a reclamation of the physical body from oppressive systems: the 'self' referred simply to the person administering the care rather than suggesting something about the type of care being administered. Later, it became a strategy for activists to avoid burnout, taking on a slightly different meaning: to tend to your own needs before you can devote energy to others'.[17]

In a contemporary, mainstream context, self-care can just as easily constitute a vague, catch-all excuse for giving in: either to your own desires, which may include the pull of buying products, or simply to buying products irrespective of whether you desired them before you were pulled. Self-care encompasses anything to do with the self (it takes a more liberal approach to 'care'). It could mean getting up early, sleeping late, getting your hair cut, getting incredibly drunk, going sober, changing your sheets, socialising when you don't want to, socialising when you do want to, staying at home when you do or don't want to; essentially, doing whatever the hell you want, or don't want, depending on the extent to which you trust yourself to have the correct instincts about whether what you want is also what you need. That this is plainly how it has been framed on social media means that it also lends itself well to heavy irony.

In 1979, on the US news show *60 Minutes*, the journalist Dan Rather explained wellness, a new movement taking off in California, as 'really the ultimate in something called "self-care"'.[18] This makes sense if, as you would have done in 1979, you take self-care at face value. But now, self-care and wellness clash: self-care is inclusionary, and wellness is exclusionary. This does not make it any less intertwined with our desire to be authentic – it just makes the aim of authenticity less clear. Self-care causes internal conflict because it is subject only to the whims of the inner self. Is it self-care to do what I instinctively want or self-care to resist?

That self-care has become synonymous with authenticity means it can function as a buzzword for brands, because advertisers know that people are desperate for guidance on becoming themselves. Here, that guidance presents not as 'you should buy this product because it, specifically, will make you more yourself', but as: 'if you *do* want to buy this product, even a little bit, you should, because the act of doing so will be an authentic expression of your true desires.' Framing the purchase of a product, whether it's a scented candle or a chocolate brownie, as 'self-care' makes the process itself feel to the consumer like an authentic act – because while in the exclusionary method, authenticity is produced by restraint, in the inclusionary method, authenticity *is* giving in.

Megan Nolan explores this idea of succumbing in her 2021 novel *Acts of Desperation*,[19] which concerns the erosion of self within a romantic relationship. Though the narrator has little sense of a fixed self – her namelessness blurs boundaries even between her and the reader – she takes solace in her ability to follow her heart and finds some semblance of identity in the very act of doing so. She writes of a friend:

Sometimes I thought about people like Lisa – people who never lost control of themselves, who never had too much of anything, who were never awake after 1 am – with something like disdain. I valued what I thought of as my free nature, my willingness to do whatever I wanted at all times, my ability to be led by whatever base physical urge was singing to me in each moment. Wasn't there some truth to the way I existed that those safer people were too timid to follow in their own lives?[20]

We instinctively agree that there is something more honest and raw about how she lives: on impulse, with intense emotions of all kinds, giving in to urges to drink and have one-off sexual encounters. But we also see how these choices lead her into an identity crisis and how her porousness makes her susceptible to erosion. There is no sense of authenticity or essence, even if her method of living is more truthful to her instincts than Lisa's seemingly sensible one. Her identity becomes bound up with the chaotic fluidity of her lifestyle, which means any efforts to be true to herself perpetuate the cycle of succumbing to impulse.

If you allow yourself to be led by people and things external to you, you are muddying the 'pure' self inside – yet you are also creating, building a self that cannot be anything other than true. The self *is* those external influences and experiences, and it is gradually built as they accumulate. In *Acts of Desperation*, the protagonist seems to acquire this sense of self through existing within the novel, and through her lack of boundaries with the world and with us. By contrast, her boyfriend, Ciaran, has cold, hard edges that cut into our softer heroine. Ciaran 'sought nothing from his surroundings. Although he didn't seem particularly happy, he seemed undeniably whole, as though his world was contained within himself.'[21] Which character, we might ask, is more authentic?

*

In popular culture we have witnessed over the past decade the birth of the 'messy heroine' – and of writing about the messy heroine. It's safe to say the messy heroine adopts the inclusionary approach: she is beautifully chaotic and artfully relatable. She has casual sex and spills drinks down herself. Her eyeliner has a tendency to smudge. She is, above all, authentic. And she became popular – via shows like *Girls*, Phoebe Waller-Bridge's *Fleabag* and Michaela Coel's *I May Destroy You* – because she is an antidote to the fantastical romcom versions of women we were used to seeing on screen.

Yet aside from her chaotic attributes, the narrative arc of the messy heroine remains very similar to that of non-messy ones. Pop culture narratives have long diverted from culminating in the hero's achievement of some elevated societal position or accomplishment of a dangerous task. Instead, the hero's quest – particularly when the hero is a woman – is simply to find and live their truth. The romcom, which so often adopts the narrative scaffolding of a fairy tale, takes an underdog heroine, runs her through various obstacles and allows her to be fully recognised by the world at the end. Her love interest also often obscures his true self somehow, and she ultimately helps him reveal it (harking back to the fairy tale 'Beauty and the Beast').

Of course, most romcom heroines are not true underdogs. If nothing else, they are always beautiful, even if their beauty is initially hidden in some way (see, in particular, *The Princess Diaries* and *The Devil Wears Prada*). The geek-to-chic makeover that occurs in so many romcoms of the 1990s and 2000s is a way of conflating the true self with beauty, homogenising the heroine's self-realisation with her self-optimisation in the same way as the exclusionary approach. Similarly, the outcome that appeases the heroine and appears to be in line with her authentic truth often happens to be committing to a stable romantic relationship with a man.

Jane Austen, whose emotionally unavailable Mr Darcy inspired not only the Mark Darcy of *Bridget Jones's Diary* but countless more icy male characters for women to melt, had something different in mind for her heroines. They are not unconcerned with questions of self, nor are they haplessly dependent on men. Trilling observes that Austen's heroines tend to aspire to a life of 'order, peace, honour and beauty which inhere in a happy and... prosperous marriage, in the sufficiency and decorum of fortunate domestic arrangements'[22] – but there is messiness in Austen's characters too. She was writing as the idea of individual authenticity was emerging, and in her characters we can feel the push and pull of society and self, withholding and succumbing. Claire Tomalin writes in *Jane Austen: A Life* that, in *Sense and Sensibility*, in which Marianne is led by impulse and feeling and her sister, Elinor, is the opposite, the author was 'considering how far society can tolerate openness, and what its effect on the individual may be'.[23] Its effect on Marianne, who wears her heart on her sleeve, is surely a kind of chaos – even aside from her romantic behaviour, her ill-advised, emotions-led country walk near the beginning of the novel causes her to slip and sprain her ankle and become ill (the event that also ultimately leads to her infatuation with the unsuitable, unavailable Mr Willoughby). Elinor, meanwhile, feels bound to '[tell] lies when politeness required it';[24] she upholds the social structure above her own 'truth'.

The messy heroine's penchant for chaos doesn't mean she is more authentic than other heroines – but it does mean that she is more likely to pursue her own authenticity at all costs, because she is less perturbed by the potential risks. The effect of her onscreen dominance is an increased urgency surrounding the inclusionary approach to authenticity: we watch these admirably imperfect women living their truths and wonder if, in order to live our own truths, we must also aspire to a life of unresolved problems and bad decisions. *Am I making a mistake by not making enough mistakes?* we might wonder, and, if so, *is that mistake authentic enough?*

*

Hardship and uncontrollable circumstances yield, of course, a strength of feeling that is conducive to the drama of TV and film. We are keen to adopt this strength of feeling for ourselves, rather than leaving it in cultural fantasy, because it also signifies authenticity – that we are truly alive. But as we see in *Acts of Desperation*, the all-encompassing approach has its own set of rules. It doesn't matter to the narrator if Lisa, her more sensible friend, lives based on her authentic desires – she still appears to be constrained by something because her lifestyle is contained and tidy. She is, somehow, impure.

The approaches of exclusion and inclusion might appear to be, respectively, bastions of discipline and liberation, with exclusion providing a set of rules by which to live and achieve purity, and inclusion inviting purity through total freedom. But both approaches also help us to see the extent to which discipline and liberation are tangled. Because while it may appear to be liberating to do whatever you want all the time, it can be a trap. It creates so much choice that you have to impose your own rules.

'The project of artistically creating the self requires not self-reflection,' writes Guignon. '… Rather, it requires an unreflective immersion in one's own life, a full participation that involves the self as a feeling and acting whole.'[25] In other words, if we are too busy becoming ourselves, we miss out on the experience of being them.

CONFESSION

In *The Will to Knowledge,*[1] the first in his four-volume study of sexuality in the West, the French philosopher Michel Foucault wrote lucidly on the history and process of confession. Confession was, he argued, the primary means by which the 'truth' about human sexuality is prone to surface, thanks to the Roman Catholic Church. 'The obligation to confess is now relayed through so many different points, is so deeply ingrained in us, that we no longer perceive it as the effect of a power that constrains us,' he wrote; 'on the contrary, it seems to us that truth, lodged in our most secret nature, "demands" only to surface; that if it fails to do so, this is because a constraint holds it in place, the violence of a power weighs it down.'[2] Writing in 1976, Foucault argued that society had long been obsessed with sex – categorising and dissecting it, implementing rules around it and, most of all, talking about it. But this obsession with talking about sex has surely now reached its peak. The very outpouring

Foucault observed means that sex is now everywhere and lacks mystery. Doubtless Foucault (who died in 1984) would have had views on the structure of sex and sexuality in the wake of the revelations of #MeToo; the LGBTQ movement, the sexual liberation of women, social media, and online pornography mean that sex has significantly less power to shock – even to be revelatory – than fifty years ago.

Yet applied more broadly, his observations about confession hold. Society is increasingly obsessed with telling, with plumbing the depths of the self for some shining epiphany. We turn ourselves inside out so others can examine and compare our inner and outer selves. Where confession was once a method of truth-production specifically about sin (and, by extension, sex), it is now a means of creating a more general, holistic authenticity. Foucault wrote that literature is 'ordered according to the infinite task of extracting from the depths of oneself, in between the words, a truth from which the very form of the confession holds out like a shimmering mirage'.[3] This is also true of social media, where the process of extraction, occurring as it does in direct parallel with the actual unfolding of your life, can never be finished. The authentic individual is not only discovered through the telling but made real. The act of expurgation on one side of the confession booth – or, in a more contemporary iteration, on the therapist's couch or while floundering in cyberspace – brings the private inner self somehow into the material world.

*

This is not to say that talking about sex has lost its ability to signal openness. The truth about sex, the rawness of it, retains its thrill – but its ubiquity in culture means that sex alone does not suffice to reveal the full extent of a person's inner world. *Fleabag*, Phoebe Waller-Bridge's breakout one-woman play and TV series, whose protagonist (the eponymous Fleabag) is often held up as the quintessential 'messy heroine', explores how sexual confession can be used both to conceal and enlighten. She not only lets us in on her most intimate sexual moments but tells us about them directly, breaking the fourth wall, sometimes during the sexual act. And yet, for all her openness, she has a big secret that she won't admit, even to us. We are left to piece it together ourselves from fragmented flashbacks, the only scenes in the show that appear to be unwillingly offered up by her, coming across her mind and our screens seemingly involuntarily. During a counselling session, Fleabag explains that she has 'spent most of my adult life using sex to deflect from the screaming void inside my empty heart' (idiosyncratically, she glances at the camera and raises an eyebrow: 'I'm good at this').[4] Authenticity in one area is used to detract from the lack of it elsewhere[5] – both in the character's inner life and within the framework of the show.

Fleabag is about control. As Foucault would have it, so is confession itself. 'The confession... [is] a ritual that unfolds within a power relationship,' he writes, 'for one does not confess without the presence (or virtual presence) of a partner who is not simply the interlocutor but the authority who requires the confession, prescribes and appreciates it, and intervenes in order to judge, punish, forgive, console, and reconcile.'[6] On these terms, the purpose of *Fleabag*'s unconventional form becomes clear. We, the viewers, are ostensibly the interlocutors for Fleabag's to-camera confessions – yet she can also control our appreciation of them by making jokes, being our friend. But that her admissions are often so relatable further tips the scale of power in her favour, not ours. Rather than making herself vulnerable, she invites us to join her in the vulnerability and inadvertently exposes something about us that might otherwise have neglected to surface. Suddenly, faced with truths we may not yet have articulated to ourselves, it is as though we are the ones confessing, and Fleabag – looking straight at us down the lens – is the intervening authority.

If a surrendering of power defines the scope of the confession, it seems Fleabag has not, at least by the end of season one, confessed much at all. It's only fitting, then, that it should be a combination of unfulfilled sexual desire, a Catholic priest and a confession booth that finally results in the revelation of Fleabag's authentic truth in the middle of season two. Fleabag's friend, The Priest, exerts a unique power over her: he cannot and will not have sex with her. His abstinence thwarts her, both in that she desperately wants to sleep with him and that by forcing her to disengage from sex, even if only physically, he removes the element of her life (and the show) which usually allows her to control the narrative. To emphasise his deep understanding of her, he is the only character in the show to notice that Fleabag is not always fully present within the characters' world. When

126

she looks to the camera to address us, he asks where she's gone, looking down the lens himself. After a season and a half of Shakespearean asides and the audience with her in her bedroom, it is in the confession booth that Fleabag finally drops her guard in a vulnerable monologue, her face turned firmly away from the camera. The Priest persuades her to tell him her 'sins' – albeit different sins from those we witnessed in the flashbacks – and she concedes in an act of surrender.

*

The confession 'produces intrinsic modifications in the person who articulates it,' wrote Foucault, '… it exonerates, redeems, and purifies him' – just like the ritual cleansing of possessions and toxins – '… it unburdens him of his wrongs, liberates him, and promises him salvation.'[7] The confession gives you the information you need to switch from your sinful path to a pious one. In Catholicism, it also exonerates simply through participation – a willingness to come forward and put yourself before God represents honesty and faith in itself.

Although confession still functions as a corrective, what defines the 'right' path is now less clear. With the decline of religious authority telling us how to behave, authenticity is, as Charles Taylor put it in *The Ethics of Authenticity*, our 'moral ideal': 'a picture of what a better or higher mode of life would be, where "better" and "higher" are defined not in terms of what we happen to desire or need, but offer a standard of what we ought to desire'.[8] The categories of 'authentic' and 'inauthentic', 'living your truth' and not living it, being happy and being unhappy, are equivalent to right and wrong. Thus, modern confession aims to bring us not into alignment with God but into alignment with our true inner selves.

The emergence of psychoanalysis in the late nineteenth century created a new way of producing truth. It was a method of inducing confession – still primarily, particularly for Foucault's interests, about sex – using 'scientifically acceptable observations'.[9] Crucially, psychoanalysis differed from Catholic confession in that it did not concern simply what the patient wanted to conceal from everyone else but 'what was hidden from himself'.[10] It gave a practical and, in some analysts' views – including Sigmund Freud's – scientific shape to unearthing the authentic self. For the twentieth-century therapist Fritz Perls, neurosis was a state caused by an 'attempt to get away from oneself'[11] – in other words, the exact opposite of authenticity – that could be cured with analysis.

Psychoanalytical theory is founded on the dichotomy of the subconscious and conscious minds, which can be likened broadly to our inner and outer selves. In Freud's theory of 'ego and id', developed in the early 1920s, the 'id' is our inner self, and the 'ego' is our outer self.[12] The rational ego attempts to control the instinctive id by repressing sexual and violent urges unacceptable in society, including what he termed the Oedipus complex: a child's sexual desire for one parent and jealousy of the other.[13] Freud described the ego as a 'facade' for the id, concealing its ugliness.[14]

Elsewhere in early psychoanalysis, the inner self was held up as desirable. Freud's contemporary Carl Jung's conception of the inner self was similarly unrestrained but altogether less sinister. Rather than imagining patients as potentially murder-ous sexual deviants, Jung thought that being in touch with the inner self involved shedding the hardened layers of repressive Judeo-Christianity that had developed over centuries and returning to humanity's primal instincts, which manifested in Dionysian raves, and oneness with the Earth.[15] Jung promised that his analysis would result in 'individuation': a self unre-strained by society, family or even God.[16] Freud, meanwhile, hoped that psychoanalysis could enable the ego to conquer the id, whose overspill of repressed emotional material mani-fested in neurotic or psychotic behaviour. Later in the twenti-eth century, the Swiss psychoanalyst Alice Miller wrote about how a lack of parental validation as a child directly leads to the creation of a 'false self', which can be dissolved in favour of authentic emotions by mourning the lost childhood.[17]

Contemporary psychoanalysis similarly promises free-dom by uniting the patient with their inner self. The writer and analyst Adam Phillips notes in his 2021 book *On Getting Better* that the psychoanalytic patient is, on an existentialist reading, often suffering from 'their fear of freedom, their refusal of their actually existing choices':[18] the purpose of the therapy, then, is to overcome that fear, remove inhibition and allow for liberation. In *The Examined Life*, the analyst Stephen Grosz writes:

> At one time or another, most of us have felt trapped by things we find ourselves thinking or doing, caught by our own impulses or foolish choices; ensnared in some unhappiness or fear; imprisoned by our own history.'[19]

The therapist facilitates the surfacing of feelings that may be driving those limiting behaviours; Grosz's language – trapped, caught, ensnared, imprisoned – makes it clear that psycho-analysis should be a process of emancipation from them. Although the model of releasing and accepting emotions is now familiar and may even seem like the only acceptable way to live, society hasn't always functioned in this way. It was Aristotle's view, for example, that having feelings 'at the right times, about the right things, toward the right people, for the right end, and in the right way, is... the best condition'.[20] Much of modern psychology is an active rejection of this idea, which now appears to be a starkly inauthentic way to live.

The inner self's inherent superiority to the outer self dominates contemporary culture. The idea that there is both a truthful subconscious and a facade guided by societal norms shimmers beneath the surface of every influencer's pseudo-profound captions, every women's magazine cover on self-care and every breakfast cereal advert that promises there is a better you just waiting to be unleashed. We rarely hear anyone advocating for changing ourselves to fit the out-side world – instead, we attempt to manifest our inner self on the outside and look for a world that will accept it. And the point of this, aside from our accepting authenticity as a worthy goal in itself, is, simply, happiness. In the 2012 film *The Pervert's Guide to Ideology*, Slavoj Žižek notes that patients no longer visit a therapist because they feel guilty about indulg-ing in excessive pleasures that go against the grain of duty or morality. Rather, they feel guilty for not enjoying themselves enough, and need help with letting loose.[21] Real life, as David

Boyle points out,[22] is to be found on holiday and not at your desk; on drugs rather than on duty. Feeling guilty for being unhappy or not seeking enough pleasure can ultimately be equated with feeling guilty for being inauthentic.

In pop psychology, which proliferates online and tends to condense complex psychoanalytic and neurological ideas into neat binaries, the aggrandisement of the inner self can result in moralising about people who do not appear to be in touch with theirs. On social media, the idea that 'everyone should get therapy' has become a doctrine for the emotionally enlightened. But dashing off such a sentiment in a tweet risks trivialising the intense emotional experiences that may actually lead someone to seek therapy. This rhetoric gives little consideration to the structural problems causing widespread distress, the structural problems preventing certain people from 'getting therapy', or the basic fact that 'therapy' – a term that encompasses a huge range of methods and objectives – cannot be homogenised into a tidy object for people to 'get'. Social media users wishing to espouse its benefits – almost always, it should be said, with genuinely good intentions – tend to portray it as a straightforward process of airing grievances about your parents and immediately feeling much better, rather than a complex, subtle experience that, depending on whether you have managed to find the right kind of treatment for your problem and a therapist you click with, might not work for you. Social media condenses emotional intelligence into platitudes, memes and pithy jokes until it eventually loses all meaning. In 2021, for example, the Instagram artist Michael Schneider, who uses letter-shaped balloons to write out wry inspirational quotes, posted an image in which the balloons read: 'Fuck nudes. Send me a dated invoice from your therapist so I know you're working on yourself.'[23]

'Working on yourself' is viewed as authentic in its own right, just like Catholic confession exonerates you simply because you turn up. Aside from the large-scale confession that occurs on the couch, sending 'a dated invoice from your therapist', or its social media equivalent, is a micro-confession that both creates and proves your authenticity. In the context of the romantic relationship in Balloon Guy's example, 'working on yourself' also signifies a kind of emotional availability. Contrary to Aristotle, a pop-psychology adage is that feelings cannot be wrong – because they are part of the inner world that is so often pushed down because of society's rules.

Of course, this idea is not inherently criticisable. It's true that the systems we inhabit – work, family, society as a whole – often require us to push away our instinctive emotional responses to events so that we can function within them. To recognise this and allow emotions to be explored and felt is, in fact, enormously significant, personally liberating, and often political – women, for example, have historically been accused of being hysterical and overly emotional as a form of oppression. Scientific advances in psychology demonstrate the efficacy of such an approach in treating mental illness and distress. To question the feelings doctrine is not to say it is necessarily wrong – it is merely to draw attention to the fact that it has become doctrine. There is undeniably a tension in something that should be liberating having become a steadfast rule of its own.

That so many of us seem so sure we need to realise our inner selves to be happy, fully functioning members of society must be because we think instinctively that the inner self is the better option. But is it always preferable? It is highly optimistic to suggest that, if we all simply go to therapy, we will emerge as authentic individuals ready to make the world a better place. In a piece on online therapy discourse for *i-D* in 2021, James Greig wrote that when the England football team lost the Euros final that year, 'the 'get some therapy' crowd were out in full force. Men, it was suggested, could be less racist, violent or drunk if only they'd give it a try.'[24] The '"get some therapy" crowd' presupposes goodness: that racism, violence or drunkenness are facets of the outer self that could be shed with the help of a confessional couch and an interlocutor. But what if some people's inner selves – as we might glean from Freud – are selfish or sadistic, or, indeed, racist or violent? Is the aim then to neutralise the undesirable traits of the inner self to make them fit better with the social structure? That surely results in something inauthentic – something that does not differ significantly from the Aristotelian idea that there is such a thing as the right feelings and a right time to feel them.

*

Like therapy, social media allows us to narrativise our own lives. As the atmosphere of social media becomes increasingly feverish and unstable and increasingly confused by irony, posting online – which has always had the implicit aim of self-realisation – has become a form of active confession. Like the priest and the therapist, followers are there to prescribe, judge and reconcile. Yet the process is subtly, crucially different: we can see a clear trajectory in the evolution of the question that confession demands from its authority. In the Catholic confession booth, we ask: am I bad? On the analyst's couch, we ask: am I mad? In self-help culture, we ask: am I happy? Online, we ask: am I authentic?

On social media, the confession process is circular. If confession has previously been used to yield some authentic truth for a greater purpose (eternal salvation, or the secular equivalent of it), here authenticity is an end in itself. It is enough simply to witness someone being sparklingly themselves by looking happy by the Grand Canyon, or by photographing their minimalist living room, or with an artfully 'chaotic' selfie, or a charismatic 'photo dump'. Truth-living is a spectacle on its own terms. The endless choice presented by the injunction to 'be yourself', whoever that may be, does not mean we need less guidance than with any other moral code. In our hungry consumption of other people's lives, we often try to find an example to follow, looking for pointers on how to live our truth and prove that we are living it.

In the mid-late 2010s, there was a surge of influencer 'authenticity'. The 2014 legislation that mandated influencers to be transparent about brand partnerships and sponsorships now seems like second nature, but at the time it shattered the whole shiny facade. A new chapter was beginning for influencers: one in which their effortless, just-like-you-but-a-bit-better act was wearing thin. The renewed appetite for authenticity, distinct from the desire for tactile organicism in the 2000s, was fuelled by a new understanding of the extent to which the internet could hide the truth. Aspiring influencers paid for followers. People catfished on Tinder. We never got to see the outtakes of a selfie session, and social media only showed the good bits of our friends' lives. And so, being well-oiled popularity machines, as quickly as influencers had sprung up looking perfect, they adapted to appear flawed. There were 'Instagram vs Reality' posts that demonstrated the efficacy of certain poses in making your body look like a model's; captions about struggles with mental health; posts about products insisting they came from a genuine belief in the brand and were therefore signposted 'not even sponsored'; a whole era of selfies with as bare a face as the subject could manage, spotless grey tracksuits and cups of herbal tea. Suddenly the aim was to prove that your life was more real than others'.

The authentic influencer pivot was analysed extensively in online journalism of the late 2010s, which noted the switch in content to, for example, photographs that showed cellulite rather than being perfectly posed or photoshopped. But less well-documented is that the 'authenticity' stemmed from the act of the confession itself. Influencers began to be more authentic not just by telling us more, or telling us different things, but by telling us specifically about their prior deceit. In 2015, by which time the Australian Instagrammer Essena O'Neill had half a million followers, she began to dismantle the structure of glossy aspiration she had created. She deleted almost all the posts from her feed and re-captioned those that remained with descriptions of what was 'really' going on when she took the pictures, in which she looked thin, happy and perfect, in the sunshine or inside expensive houses. In hindsight, it should surprise no one that she – along with many people like her – was anxious, depressed and image-obsessed. Under one smiling selfie, she confessed that it had taken fifty attempts before settling on the right photo. 'THERE IS NOTHING REAL ABOUT THIS',[25] she wrote – and changed her Instagram name to 'Social Media Is Not Real Life' before removing her account entirely a few years later.

As online celebrities competed to reveal just how much of themselves they'd previously been hiding, the followers were captivated: either as sincere believers taking solace in the fantastical nature of what had seemed like an unachievably perfect world, or watching at a remove as these endless layers were dissected and exposed. The Instagrammer Tavi Gevinson wrote a viral piece for *The Cut* in 2019 in which she admitted that 'I came to see my shareable self as the authentic one and buried any tendencies that might threaten her likability so deep down I forgot they even existed'.[26] The article came just six days after *The Cut* had gone viral with a now-infamous influencer authenticity exposé: 'I Was Caroline Calloway'.[27]

Caroline Calloway's Wikipedia page reads: 'Caroline Gotschall Calloway (born December 5, 1991) is an American internet celebrity known for posting Instagram photos with long captions', a sentence so knowingly disparaging that it could have been written by Calloway herself. The question of Calloway's authorship of her persona was at the heart of *The Cut*'s article. It was written by Natalie Beach, Calloway's former friend, who revealed that she had been behind Caroline's famous 'long captions' all along. Calloway had already been exposed as a 'scammer' for her never-published memoir (which Beach also tried to help her write) and a cancelled US tour of 'creativity workshops', which were supposed to teach attendees how to live their 'best life', and for which she had failed to book any venues (despite attendees having paid $165 a ticket). The article simply revealed another layer of deceit. Calloway's whole thing was to be authentic, documenting her wild, flawed self for all to see by building her own narrative. This was not just inauthenticity like Essena O'Neill's – it was inauthenticity squared. Twitter inhaled it, buzzing on truth and lies. Beach's article was excoriating, but it was also being commentated on in live time by Calloway herself. In a series of compulsive-seeming Instagram posts, she recounted her version of several of the events Beach had described and also documented her reaction to the piece itself, ensuring this event was itself incorporated into her never-ending self-narrative.

O'Neill and other influencers in the classic mould were keen to draw a line between Instagram and reality, authentic and inauthentic – maintaining a clean-cut, neatly imagined world of good and bad. They came clean in the same way public figures always have, with a straightforward confessional – an admission of wrongdoing or diversion from the norm that, in its humanness, sets them back on the right path.

This often occurs in sport: several professional tennis players – such as Naomi Osaka and Emma Raducanu – have recently been candid about their mental health, which is particularly significant in a game that relies so heavily on mental stamina. After taking a hiatus from boxing, Tyson Fury revealed his struggles with depression and substance addiction. When he returned to the public eye, he said: 'This time I want to be myself, I don't want to play a character anymore'.[28]

Conversely, that Calloway simply rode the wave of her exponentially increasing inauthenticity somehow enabled her to appear even more authentic in an all-encompassing, chaotic sense. After the disastrous workshops were reported on online, she self-styled as a 'scammer', twisting the characterisation into irony, so its truth became irrelevant to its meaning. She set up a new workshop event in 2019 called 'The Scam'.[29] She retweets comments about herself obsessively so that everyone else's observations and jokes about her appear as part of her own feed, with her as the author. In 2019, with nothing left to confess, she joined the adult content platform OnlyFans and began to offer the final part of herself for exposure – her body – sharing nude photos there and on Twitter. Jean-Jacques Rousseau's 1782 text *Confessions*, which is fundamental to the emergence of authenticity as an idea, captures the essence of the Calloway project in that Rousseau was determined that his work would be comprehensive above all else. It would contain everything about him, including his innermost thoughts and feelings, and therefore yield a perfect picture of who he really was. 'Assemble round thy throne an innumerable throng of my fellow-mortals,' he wrote, 'let them listen to my confessions, let them blush at my depravity, let them tremble at my sufferings; let each in his turn expose with equal sincerity the failings, the wanderings of his heart'.[30]

And just as we blush at the depravity of Calloway, we expose the failings and wanderings of our own hearts. Plenty of the online confessions we make are overtly exposing or even shameful. 'One goes about telling, with the greatest precision,' says Foucault, 'whatever is most difficult to tell.'[31] Or, in the words of the Romantic novelist Nathaniel Hawthorne: 'Be true! Be true! Be true! Show freely to the world, if not your worst, yet some trait by which the worst may be inferred!'[32] Our confessions that demand reconciliation might involve a crying selfie or an admission of neurosis (perhaps with a well-placed therapy meme). Increasingly an 'ugly' aesthetic pervades Instagram: a non-airbrushed, chaotic antidote to the smoothed-over scenes of the 2010s, but also a deliberate positioning of authentic selves asking to be validated.

There is also a greater propensity for us to engage in this self-expurgation than ever before. The communication model online has in recent years become more openly confessional. We once showed, and now we actively tell. The video-only platform TikTok has grown astronomically since its launch in 2016, and other social media platforms, particularly Instagram, lean increasingly on camera-facing video features. Instagram's 'Stories' feature, launched in 2016, borrowed from the disappearing-content model popularised by Snapchat. It was a drive for authenticity in its transience, incentivising users to share more candid moments safe in the knowledge they would not be immortalised. It also encouraged the audience-facing video format previously limited to YouTube vlogging. Users can spout whatever is on their minds to the front camera of their phones and an invisible audience. Captions similarly ramble into Calloway-esque essays, a picture of an outfit being prime territory for recounting your life story.

Even if we are not consciously or actively telling, micro-confessions happen constantly on social media. One of the most common and consistent is the somewhat exhausting use of irony that pervades online interactions (the only thing more exhausting is attempting a sincerity that does not quite come off due to the natural communication barrier created by the screen). Irony online is how we accept the paradox embodied in trying to be authentic. The ironic 'lol' used as a suffix to signify lightness in online communication – 'I want to kill myself lol' – also signifies self-awareness. 'Including "lol" indicates a second layer of meaning to be found, telling the recipient to look beyond the literal words you're saying,' writes Gretchen McCulloch in *Because Internet*, her 2019 book on online linguistics.[33] Crucially, it tells the recipient that you already know what that second layer of meaning is: that you are aware of the authentic truth underneath the necessarily inauthentic – which is to say, unreal – virtual interaction.

To be truly authentic online – to transcend the realm of performative candidness and vacuous sentimentality – we enter a state of hyper-self-awareness. This doesn't just mean that we agonise over captions, what to post and what not to post, but that we do so with an intense pressure to know exactly what the post looks like to others. If we succeed in this, it shows that we are so self-aware that we understand every element of our personality that may be intentionally or unintentionally expressed in what we upload to the internet. Ironically, by pre-empting whatever response someone else might have, we ensure we cannot be truly exposed. Posting photos of yourself with the caption 'Shameless selfie' demonstrates that you are all too aware of its potential shamefulness. Tweets prefaced 'Sorry to be sincere but' or '*earnest tweet alert!*' show that you understand that genuine, unacknowledged sincerity is the most deeply uncool trait to possess on the internet (although, like true 'basicness', it also conveys enviable freedom – a genuine, accidental authenticity). Another, less specific option – along the lines of 'for real' or 'real talk' – is usually reserved for something banal whose importance has been exaggerated for comic effect ('real talk – this is the cutest dog i've ever seen'), reversing the irony so that what we think is going to be a serious confession is another pointless, yet relatable, observation. Hyperbole is an extension of confession: proclaiming strong feelings about things is a way of turning ourselves inside-out and proving the intensity of our inner world.

Most of all, irony and outright self-awareness subtly affect the power dynamic of online interaction. Though both signify authenticity, they ultimately limit the potential for it to occur: they take power away from the necessarily authoritative followers and observers and deaden the impact of the potential confession. The serious and unserious become indistinguishable: a statement about being depressed can be delivered in the same tone as a piece of celebrity gossip. This inscrutability means that we do not always know what is a confession and what is just a joke, what is sincere and what is ironic – and ultimately what is real and what is not.

*

To the non-religious, the Catholic Church's model of confession smacks of disingenuousness. You can do whatever you want, and as long as you go and tell a priest about it, you'll still go to heaven? Do you even have to be sorry? Do you actually want to confess, or is it just what you're supposed to do? Yet similar questions could be asked of some who partake in its modern-day secular equivalents. Do you really want to change, or is going to therapy just what you're supposed to do? Do you actually know who you are, or is sharing yourself online just what you're supposed to do?

Foucault's framework reveals perhaps the most important dynamic in authenticity culture. In all forms of confession, there is also a power relationship within the self: between our inner self and our performed, confessed self. As part of the self is actualised through confession, another part of it – the thinking mind, the 'I' that is bound up in our very existence, the one that necessarily stays inside – can watch it.

When the therapist sits in silence, offering nothing, we are supposed to let our words hang in the air and allow the truth to sink in through the hole in our psyche created by their excavation. Online, too, our followers only account for so much. We often find ourselves looking through our own social media feeds to see what they see, to assess the image of ourselves we have projected to others. When we do this, we are looking at our own 'highlight reel', the perfectly constructed self we have created for the world to know. But in this process of self-realisation, we have become our own interlocutor. We constantly confess, and then ask our inner selves for feedback on the object the confession has created. *Is this who I am?*

If any self we put out into the world is subject to the same analysis and questioning, to the same rules of performance, is being authentic materially different from being inauthentic? We are gripped by the search for consistency between our inner and outer selves, but how do we know when that search is complete? Even when our self is realised on social media or elsewhere, we cannot truly know – it does not have the same quality, the same timbre, as whatever happens on the inside. What we are talking about is a feeling – a feeling of satisfaction, wholeness, and contentment. Ultimately, a feeling of happiness.

Foucault asks us to consider whether 'the obligation to conceal [sex] was but another aspect of the duty to admit to it'.[34] The same could be asked of the self: does the idea of a hidden inner truth derive from, rather than give rise to, the notion that self-realisation is more important than anything else? Is our categorising of inner and outer, authentic and inauthentic, simply a way of propelling this never-ending quest? What would happen if we turned our attention elsewhere? If we said, 'this is not who I am' – and did not try to prove who we were instead?

NOTES

INTRODUCTION

1   Trilling, Lionel, *Sincerity and Authenticity* (Cambridge: Harvard University Press, 1971).

2   Shakespeare, William, *Hamlet*, Act I, Scene 3, l. 78.

3   Guignon, Charles, *On Being Authentic* [ebook] (London: Routledge, 2004).

4   Guignon, *On Being Authentic*, p. 4.

5   Rousseau, Jean-Jacques, *Confessions* [ebook] (London: Reeves & Turner, 1861, first published 1782).

6   Taylor, Charles, *The Ethics of Authenticity* (USA: Harvard University Press, 2018, first published 1991).

7   Dabiri, Emma, *What White People Can Do Next* (London: Penguin Random House, 2021).

CELEBRITY

1   Dyer, Richard, *Stars* (London: British Film Institute 1998, first published 1979) p. 45.

2   Alberoni, Francesco, 'The powerless "Elite": theory and sociological research on the phenomenon of the stars', in Redmond, S., and Holmes, S., eds. *Stardom and Celebrity: A Reader* (Thousand Oaks, CA: Sage 2007).

3   Debord, Guy, *Society of the Spectacle* (first published 1967, Pattern Books 2020) pp. 32–33.

4   Boorstin, Daniel J., *The Image: A Guide to Pseudo-Events in America*, 50th anniversary edition (New York: Vintage, 2012, first published 1962) pp. 45, 57–58.

5   Zimmer, Ben, 'The Origins of "Relatable"', *New York Times* (13 August 2010), https://www.nytimes.com/2010/08/15/magazine/15onlanguage.html. Accessed 13 July 2022.

6   Lee, Kate, 'Stars, they're just like us', medium.com (27 February 2013), https://medium.com/@kate/stars-theyre-just-like-us-186c59d740eb. Accessed 13 July 2022.

7   *The Simple Life*, Bunim-Murray Productions/20th Century Fox.

8   Beyoncé (@beyonce), 'Sir Carter and Rumi 1 month today...', Instagram (14 July 2017), https://www.instagram.com/p/BWg8ZWyghFy/?taken-by=beyonce&hl=en. Accessed 13 July 2022.

9   Fecteau, Jessica, 'Julianne Moore on Jennifer Lawrence: "She's a Genuinely Authentic Individual"', *People.com* (2 December 2015), https://people.com/movies/julianne-moore-on-jennifer-lawrence-shes-a-genuinely-authentic-individual/. Accessed 13 July 2022.

10 Dawson Hoff, Victoria, 'Jennifer Lawrence's Singing Voice is Awesomely Awful', *Elle* (13 November 2014), https://www.elle.com/culture/celebrities/news/a19907/jennifer-lawrence-cannot-sing/. Accessed 13 July 2022.

11 Rose, Rebecca, 'Just When You Think Jennifer Lawrence Can't Fit Another Marshmallow In Her Mouth, She Surprises You', *Cosmopolitan*, 2 October 2015. https://www.cosmopolitan.com/entertainment/news/a47139/just-when-you-think-jennifer-

lawrence-cant-fit-another-marshmallow-in-her-mouth-she-surprises-you/. Accessed 13 July 2022.

12 Robehmed, Natalie, 'The World's Highest Paid Actresses 2015: Jennifer Lawrence Leads with \$52 million', *Forbes*, 20 August 2015, https://www.forbes.com/sites/natalierobehmed/2015/08/20/the-worlds-highest-paid-actresses-2015-jennifer-lawrence-leads-with-52-million/?sh=5e9252ae4c0a. Accessed 14 July 2022.

13 Van Meter, Jonathan, 'Jennifer Lawrence Is Determined, Hilarious, and – Above All – *Real*', *Vogue*, 11 November 2015. https://www.vogue.com/article/jennifer-lawrence-december-2015-cover-hunger-games. Accessed 20 July 2022.

14 Reed, Sam, 'The 5 Most Relatable Moments from Jennifer Lawrence's *Vogue* Interview', *The Hollywood Reporter*, 12 November 2015. https://www.hollywoodreporter.com/news/general-news/jennifer-lawrence-covers-vogue-839697/. Accessed 20 July 2022.

15 'Celebrity Family Feud' on *Saturday Night Live*, Season 41, Episode 15, NBC (3 December 2016).

16 Holmes, Sally, 'An Ode To Jennifer Lawrence Being Her Most Jennifer Lawrence Self On The "Hunger Games" Red Carpet', *Elle*, 20 November 2015. https://www.elle.com/culture/celebrities/news/g27314/jennifer-lawrence-hunger-games-red-carpet/. Accessed 20 July 2022.

17 Dyer, *Stars*, p. 35.

18 Styles, Ruth, 'Kim Kardashian kept "leaked" sex tapes in a Nike shoebox under her bed…', *MailOnline*, 5 May 2022, https://www.dailymail.co.uk/news/article-10778471/Kim-Kardashian-second-sex-tape-Ray-J-says-hits-claim-planned-leak-it.html. Accessed 14 July 2022.

19 *Keeping Up With The Kardashians*, E! (2007–2021).

20 In 'Spring 2020 Transition' on 'The Duke and Duchess of Sussex' (https://sussexroyal.com/spring-2020-transition/): 'The Royal Family respect and understand the wish of the Duke and Duchess

of Sussex to live a more independent life as a family, by removing the supposed 'public interest' justification for media intrusion into their lives.' Accessed 20 July 2022.

21 *Oprah with Meghan and Harry*, CBS (first aired 7 March 2021).

22 'Meghan and Harry interview: I didn't want to be alive any more, duchess says', *BBC News*, 8 March 2021. https://www.bbc.co.uk/news/uk-56316850. Accessed 21 July 2022.

23 Morgan, Piers, 'It takes a staggering degree of narcissism to play hard-done-by victims from your Californian mansion...', *MailOnline*, 1 March 2021, https://www.dailymail.co.uk/news/article-9312509/PIERS-MORGAN-service-Meghan-Harry-know-self-service.html. Accessed 21 July 2022.

24 Couric, Katie, 'Kim Kardashian: We Can't Keep Up!', *Glamour*, 2 January 2011. https://www.glamour.com/story/kim-kardashian-we-cant-keep-up, accessed 14 July 2022.

25 'Free Khloé', *Keeping Up With the Kardashians*, Season 3, Episode 1 (first aired 8 March 2009).

26 'Lip Service', *Keeping Up With the Kardashians*, Season 10, Episode 9 (first aired 10 May 2015).

27 Robehmed, Natalie, 'At 21, Kylie Jenner Becomes the Youngest Self-Made Billionaire Ever', *Forbes* (5 March 2019) https://www.forbes.com/sites/natalierobehmed/2019/03/05/at-21-kylie-jenner-becomes-the-youngest-self-made-billionaire-ever/?sh=512a3f852794. Accessed 14 July 2022.

28 Peterson-Withorn, Chase, and Berg, Madeline, 'Inside Kylie Jenner's Web of Lies – and Why She's No Longer a Billionaire', *Forbes* (updated 1 June 2020), https://www.forbes.com/sites/chasewithorn/2020/05/29/inside-kylie-jennerss-web-of-lies-and-why-shes-no-longer-a-billionaire/?sh=1a649f7f25f7. Accessed 14 July 2022.

29 *Forbes*, 'The New Mobile Moguls: How anyone with a following can cash in...', cover of issue dated 26 July 2016.

30 Kardashian, Kim, @kimkardashian, '#NotBadForAGirl WithNoTalent…', Twitter (11 June 2016), https://twitter.com/Kim Kardashian/status/752522458054307841. Accessed 31 July 2022.

31 *The Diary of a CEO with Steven Bartlett* [podcast], Episode 110: 'Molly Mae: How She Became Creative Director Of PLT At 22' (13 December 2021).

32 Wagmeister, Elizabeth, '"Money Always Matters": The Kardashians Tell All About Their New Reality TV Reign' [interview], *Variety* (9 March 2022), https://variety.com/2022/tv/features/kardashians-hulu-kris-kim-khloe-1235198939/. Accessed 31 July 2022.

33 West, Kanye, 'Famous', *The Life of Pablo* (Getting Out Our Dreams II, LLC, distributed by Def Jam, a division of UMG Recordings Inc., 2016) [Apple Music].

34 Trilling, *Sincerity and Authenticity*, p. 9.

35 Leszkiewicz, Anna, 'Kim Kardashian vs Taylor Swift: a battle of two PR styles', *New Statesman* (18 July 2016), https://www.newstatesman.com/culture/music-theatre/2016/07/kim-kardashian-vs-taylor-swift-battle-two-pr-styles, accessed 14 July 2022.

36 As cited in Leszkiewicz, 'Kim Kardashian vs Taylor Swift…'.

37 Syme, Rachel, 'The Shapeshifter', *New York Times Magazine* (3 October 2018), https://www.nytimes.com/interactive/2018/10/03/magazine/lady-gaga-movie-star-is-born.html. Accessed 14 July 2022.

38 Syme, 'The Shapeshifter'.

39 Syme, 'The Shapeshifter'.

40 MacInnes, Paul, 'Beyoncé? We think you mean Sasha Fierce', *Guardian* (24 October 2008), https://www.theguardian.com/music/2008/oct/24/beyonce-sasha-fierce. Accessed 14 July 2022.

41 Swift, Taylor, 'Look What You Made Me Do', *Reputation* (Big Machine, 2017) [Apple Music].

42 *An American Family*, PBS (11 January 1973).

43 As cited in Le Vine, Lauren, 'Some Of You Asked Us To Stop Writing About The Kardashians – This Is Our Response', *Refinery29* (30 July 2015), https://www.refinery29.com/en-gb/2015/07/199418/kardashian-family-pop-culture-relevance. Accessed 31 July 2022.

44 Lim, Dennis, 'Reality-TV Originals, In Drama's Lens', *New York Times* (17 April 2011), https://www.nytimes.com/2011/04/17/arts/television/hbos-cinema-verite-looks-at-american-family.html. Accessed 11 April 2021.

45 Gamson, Joshua, 'The Unwatched Life Is Not Worth Living: The Elevation of the Ordinary in Celebrity Culture', JSTOR, *PMLA*, vol. 126, no. 4, 2011, p. 1065. www.jstor.org/stable/41414175. Accessed 27 Feb. 2021.

46 Gamson, 'The Unwatched Life…', p. 1065.

47 O'Neill, Lauren, '"Move Over Britney, I'm Coming to Vegas" – Gemma Collins Talks Life Onscreen and Beyond', *Vice* (13 October 2020), https://www.vice.com/en/article/7kp5ed/move-over-britney-im-coming-to-vegas-gemma-collins-talks-life-onscreen-and-beyond. Accessed 14 July 2022.

48 O'Neill, '"Move Over Britney…"'.

49 Boorstin, *The Image*, p. 48.

50 Boorstin, *The Image*, p. 61.

ART

1 Sudjic, Olivia, *Exposure* (London: Peninsula Press, 2018).

2 Sudjic, *Exposure*, p. 86.

3 Sudjic, *Exposure*, p. 85.

4 Sudjic, *Exposure*, pp. 112–113.

5 Choi, Susan, *Trust Exercise*, (London: Serpent's Tail, 2020, first published 2019), p. 48.

6 Choi, *Trust Exercise*, p. 132.

7 Choi, *Trust Exercise*, p. 191.

8 'Between You And Me: A Correspondence on Autofiction in Contemporary Literature between Isabelle Graw and Brigitte Weingart', *Texte zur Kunst*, no. 115 (September 2019): 46, cited in Handahl, Philipp, 'The Decade of Magical Thinking: How Autofiction Reinvents Criticism', *Mousse* (7 July 2020), https://www.moussemagazine.it/magazine/autofiction-reinvents-criticism-philipp-hindahl-2020/. Accessed 14 July 2022.

9 Lawrence, D. H., *Sons and Lovers* (Ware: Wordsworth, 1993, first published 1913).

10 Choi, *Trust Exercise*, p. 133.

11 Trilling, *Sincerity and Authenticity*, p. 7.

12 Joyce, James, *A Portrait of the Artist as a Young Man*, as cited in Trilling, *Sincerity and Authenticity*, p. 7.

13 Eliot, T. S., 'Tradition and the Individual Talent', as cited in Trilling, *Sincerity and Authenticity*, p. 7.

14 Lee, Hermione, 'Philip Roth: The Art of Fiction No. 84' [interview], *Paris Review* (Issue 93, Fall 1984), https://www.theparisreview.org/interviews/2957/the-art-of-fiction-no-84-philip-roth. Accessed 16 July 2022.

15 Kafka, Franz, *Letters to Felice*, trans. James Stern and Elizabeth Duckworth (New York: Schocken, 1973), cited in Corngold, Stanley, *Franz Kafka: The Necessity of Form* (Cornell University Press, 1988), *JSTOR*, http://www.jstor.org/stable/10.7591/j.ctt207g62q. Accessed 16 July 2022.

16 As cited in Waldman, Katy, 'Who Owns a Story?' [article], *New Yorker* (17 April 2019), https://www.newyorker.com/books/under-review/who-owns-a-story-trust-exercise-susan-choi. Accessed 16 July 2022.

17 Friedman, Ann, 'Who Gets to Speak and Why: A conversation with Chris Kraus' [interview], *The Cut* (22 June 2017), https://

www.thecut.com/2017/06/chris-kraus-in-conversation-with-ann-friedman.html. Accessed 16 July 2022.

18 Scutts, Joanna, 'Jenny Offill: "I no longer felt like it was my fight"' [interview], *Guardian* (8 February 2020), https://www.theguardian.com/books/2020/feb/08/jenny-offill-interview. Accessed 16 July 2022.

19 Sudjic, *Exposure*, p. 65.

20 Handahl, 'The Decade of Magical Thinking'.

21 Oyler, Lauren, *Fake Accounts* (London: 4th Estate 2021).

22 Oyler, *Fake Accounts*, p. 118.

23 Oyler, *Fake Accounts*, p. 62.

24 Roupenian, Kristen, 'Cat Person' [short story], *New Yorker* (4 December 2017), https://www.newyorker.com/magazine/2017/12/11/cat-person. Accessed 16 July 2022.

25 Nowicki, Alexis, '"Cat Person" and Me' [article], *Slate* (8 July 2021), https://slate.com/human-interest/2021/07/cat-person-kristen-roupenian-viral-story-about-me.html. Accessed 16 July 2022.

26 Treisman, Deborah, 'Kristen Roupenian on the Self-Deceptions of Dating' [interview], *New Yorker* (4 December 2017), https://www.newyorker.com/books/this-week-in-fiction/fiction-this-week-kristen-roupenian-2017-12-11. Accessed 16 July 2022.

27 Engel Bromwich, Jonah, '"Cat Person" in the New Yorker: A Discussion With the Author' [interview], *New York Times* (11 December 2017), https://www.nytimes.com/2017/12/11/books/cat-person-new-yorker.html?. Accessed 16 July 2022.

28 Nowicki, '"Cat Person" and Me'.

29 Kolker, Robert, 'Who Is The Bad Art Friend?' [article], *New York Times* (5 October 2021), https://www.nytimes.com/2021/10/05/magazine/dorland-v-larson.html. Accessed 16 July 2022.

30 Nowicki, '"Cat Person" and Me'.

31 Cummins, Jeanine, *American Dirt* (UK: Tinder Press, 2020).

32 As cited in Hampton, Rachelle, 'Why Everyone's Talking About

American Dirt' [article], *Slate* (21 January 2020), https://slate.com/culture/2020/01/american-dirt-book-controversy-explained.html. Accessed 31 July 2022.

33 Kinchen, Rosie, 'Brick Lane author Monica Ali on burnout and writer's block: "I call it depression"' [interview], *The Times* (30 January 2022), https://www.thetimes.co.uk/article/brick-lane-author-monica-ali-on-burnout-and-writers-block-i-call-it-depression-30lzc5f7v#:~:text=%E2%80%9CIt%20was%20a%20major%20loss,when%20I%20wasn't%20writing. Accessed 16 July 2022.

34 @melindammme, 'the list of things Lana Del Rey invented', Twitter (18 September 2019), now deleted. Via *BuzzFeed*, https://www.buzzfeed.com/jonmichaelpoff/funny-tweets-from-this-month-sept-2019. Accessed 30 July 2022.

35 Powers, Ann, 'Lana Del Rey lives in America's messy subconscious' [article], *NPR* (4 September 2019), https://www.npr.org/2019/09/04/757545360/lana-del-rey-lives-in-americas-messy-subconscious?t=1657986925951. Accessed 16 July 2022.

36 Trilling, *Sincerity and Authenticity*, p. 8.

37 Powers, 'Lana Del Rey…'.

38 Powers, 'Lana Del Rey…'.

39 Lana Del Rey (@LanaDelRey), 'Here's a little sidenote on your piece…', Twitter (5 September 2019), now deleted, accessed via *PopCrave*, https://popcrave.com/lana-del-reys-letter-to-critics-met-with-backlash-online-heres-why/, 31 July 2022.

40 Quoted in Snapes, Laura, 'The ordinary boys: how Ed Sheeran-inspired troubadours swept the charts' [article], *Guardian* (15 March 2019), https://www.theguardian.com/music/2019/mar/15/ordinary-boys-ed-sheeran-inspired-troubadours-swept-charts. Accessed 16 July 2022.

41 Rodrigo, Olivia, 'drivers license' (Official Video) (Geffen Records, 2021), https://www.youtube.com/watch?v=ZmDBbnmKpqQ. Accessed 31 July 2022.

42 Now deleted, as cited in Robidoux, Brandy, 'The Original Lyrics of "Drivers License" May Mean It's Not About Sabrina Carpenter After All', *Elite Daily* (13 January 2021), https://www.elitedaily.com/p/this-early-version-of-olivia-rodrigos-drivers-license-may-mean-its-not-about-sabrina-carpenter-55263869. Accessed 31 July 2022.

43 Rodrigo, Olivia, 'good 4 u' (Official Video) (Geffen Records, 2021), https://www.youtube.com/watch?v=gNi_6U5Pm_o. Accessed 31 July 2022.

44 Rodrigo, Olivia, 'brutal', *Sour*.

45 Choi, *Trust Exercise*.

PRODUCT

1 Boyle, David, *Authenticity: Brands, Fakes, Spin and the Lust for Real Life*, second edition (London: Harper Perennial 2004, first published 2003).

2 Boyle, *Authenticity*, p. 21.

3 'The Ronseal Phrase' on Ronseal.com, https://www.ronseal.com/the-ronseal-phrase/. Accessed 24 July 2022.

4 Klein, Naomi, *No Logo* (London: Flamingo 2001, first published 1999), p. 3.

5 Klein, *No Logo* p. 24.

6 Dangoor, Reuben, and Riley, Raf, 'Being A Dickhead's Cool', YouTube, 9 September 2010. https://www.youtube.com/watch?v=lVmmYMwFj1I

7 Schultz, Howard, *Pour Your Heart Into It* (New York: Hyperion 1997) p. 5, as cited in Klein, *No Logo*, p. 20.

8 Scott Bedbury as quoted in the *New York Times*, 20 October 1997, as cited in Klein, *No Logo*, p. 20.

9 Malone, Noreen, 'What Do You *Really* Mean When You Say "Basic Bitch"?' [article], the *Cut* (14 October 2014) https://www.

thecut.com/2014/10/what-do-you-really-mean-by-basic-bitch.
html. Accessed 16 July 2022.

10 Lange, Maggie, 'The "Basic Bitch": Who Is She?' [article], the *Cut*
(10 April 2014) https://www.thecut.com/2014/04/basic-bitch-
who-is-she.html. Accessed 25 July 2022.

11 James, William, *The Principles of Psychology*, Vol. 1 (New York:
Henry Holt 1890), cited in Belk, Russell W., 'Possessions and
the Extended Self', *Journal of Consumer Research*, vol. 15, no. 2,
1988, pp. 139–68. *JSTOR*, http://www.jstor.org/stable/2489522.
Accessed 17 Jul. 2022.

12 Nike advert, 1984, quoted in Badenhausen, Kurt, 'Michael Jordan
Has Made Over $1bn from Nike...' [article], *Forbes* (3 May 2020),
https://www.forbes.com/sites/kurtbadenhausen/2020/05/03/
michael-jordans-1-billion-nike-endorsement-is-the-biggest-
bargain-in-sports/?sh=2e64197b6136. Accessed 25 July
2022.

13 Patton, Phil, 'The Selling of Michael Jordan' [article], *New York
Times* (9 November 1986), https://archive.nytimes.com/www.
nytimes.com/library/sports/basketball/110986bkn-jordan.html.
Accessed 25 July 2022.

14 'Number of brand sponsored influencer posts on Instagram
from 2016 to 2020', Statista, https://www.statista.com/
statistics/693775/instagram-sponsored-influencer-content/.
Accessed 23 July 2022.

15 Boyle, *Authenticity*, p. 162.

16 Boyle, *Authenticity* p. 162.

17 Data from Influencer Marketing Hub, via Oberlo, https://
www.oberlo.com/statistics/influencer-marketing-market-size.
Accessed 31 July 2022.

18 Matter Communications survey, as reported in *BusinessWire*
(26 May 2020), https://www.businesswire.com/news/home/
20200526005058/en/Matter-Survey-Reveals-Consumers-Find-

Influencers-More-Helpful-and-Trustworthy-than-Brands-During-the-Pandemic. Accessed 31 July 2022.

19 For further reading on this topic see Tolentino, Jia, 'Always Be Optimising', in *Trick Mirror* (London: 4th Estate 2019).

20 Taylor, *The Ethics of Authenticity*, p. 17.

IDENTITY

1 Davies, William, 'New-Found Tribes' [review], *London Review of Books*, vol. 43, no. 3, 4 February 2021, https://www.lrb.co.uk/the-paper/v43/n03/william-davies/new-found-tribes. Accessed 17 July 2022.

2 Fukuyama, Francis, *Identity* (London: Profile Books 2018).

3 Gouldner, Alvin W, 'Cosmopolitans and Locals: Toward an Analysis of Latent Social Roles — I', *Administrative Science Quarterly 2* no. 3 (December 1957) p. 282–283, cited in Appiah, Kwame Anthony, *The Lies That Bind: Rethinking Identity* (London: Profile Books 2019), p. 5.

4 Erikson, Erik, *Childhood and Society*, 2nd edition (New York: WW Norton 1985; originally published 1950), p. 282, cited in Appiah, *The Lies That Bind*, p. 4.

5 Hall, Stuart, 'Cultural Identity and Diaspora' (1990) in Gilroy, Paul and Wilson Gilmore, Ruth (eds.), *Selected Writings on Race and Difference* (Duke University Press, 2021), pp. 257–71. *JSTOR*, https://doi.org/10.2307/j.ctv1hhj1b9.17. Accessed 28 July 2022.

6 Hall, 'Cultural Identity and Diaspora'.

7 Sarkar, Ash, 'Why we need to pause before claiming cultural appropriation' [article], *The Guardian* (29 April 2019), https://www.theguardian.com/commentisfree/2019/apr/29/cultural-appropriation-racial-oppression-exploitation-colonialism. Accessed 17 July 2022.

8 Dabiri, *What White People Can Do Next*.

9 Dabiri, *What White People Can Do Next*, p. 4.

10 Dabiri, *What White People Can Do Next*, p. 46.

11 Dabiri, *What White People Can Do Next*, p. 24.

12 Ratajkowski, Emily, *My Body* (New York: Metropolitan Books 2021), p. 90.

13 Laing, RD, *The Divided Self*, 3rd edition (London: Penguin Books 1990; originally published 1960), pp. 51–52.

14 Eatwell, Roger, and Goodwin, Matthew, *National Populism: The Revolt Against Liberal Democracy* (UK: Penguin Random House 2018), p. 27.

15 Eatwell and Goodwin, *National Populism*, p. 28.

16 Eatwell and Goodwin, *National Populism*, p. 35.

17 Olusoga, David, 'The "statue wars" must not distract us from a reckoning with racism' [article], *Guardian* (14 June 2020), https://www.theguardian.com/global/2020/jun/14/statue-wars-must-not-distract-reckoning-with-racism-david-olusoga. Accessed 17 July 2022.

18 Olusoga, 'The "statue wars"…'.

19 Olusoga, 'The "statue wars"…'.

20 Hussain, Danyal, '"Are they worried about Jane Austen fans?": Statue defenders draw scorn as they stand in front of sculpture of writer George Eliot during Black Lives Matter protest' [article], *MailOnline* (16 June 2020), https://www.dailymail.co.uk/news/article-8426005/Statue-defenders-stand-sculpture-writer-George-Eliot-Black-Lives-Matter-demo.html. Accessed 17 July 2022.

21 Laing, *The Divided Self*, p. 52.

22 Butler, Judith, *Gender Trouble*, 4th edition (Abingdon: Routledge, 2007; originally published 1990).

23 'List of LGBTQ+ terms', Stonewall, https://www.stonewall.org.uk/help-advice/faqs-and-glossary/list-lgbtq-terms. Accessed 31 July 2022.

24 Cited in Stock, Kathleen, *Material Girls* (London: Fleet 2021), p. 27.

25 de Beauvoir, Simone, *The Second Sex*, trans. E. M. Parsley (New York: Vintage, 1973), p. 301, as cited in Butler, *Gender Trouble*, p. 11.

26 Butler, *Gender Trouble*, p. 11.

27 Stock, *Material Girls*, p. 27.

28 Stock, *Material Girls*, p. 15.

29 Laing, *The Divided Self*, p. 52.

30 *The Combahee River Collective Statement* (United States, 2015, original statement dated 1977). Web Archive: https://www.loc.gov/item/lcwaN0028151/. Accessed 28 July 2022.

31 *The Combahee River Collective Statement*.

32 Fukuyama, *Identity*, p. 37.

33 See Fukuyama, *Identity*, pp. 26; 163.

34 Appiah, *The Lies That Bind*, p. 218.

PURITY

1 'Pilot', *Girls*, Season 1, Episode 1 (first aired 15 April 2012).

2 Guignon, *On Being Authentic* [ebook], p. 67.

3 See Guignon, *On Being Authentic*, pp. 4–5.

4 'How Religious Are British People?' [survey], YouGov, https://yougov.co.uk/topics/lifestyle/articles-reports/2020/12/29/how-religious-are-british-people. Accessed 28 July 2022.

5 Guignon, *On Being Authentic*, p. 37.

6 McGraw, Phil, *Self Matters: Creating Your Life from the Inside Out* [ebook] (Free Press, 2001), p. 28.

7 McGraw, *Self Matters*, p. 29.

8 McGraw, *Self Matters*, p. 30.

9 Kondo, Marie, *The Life-Changing Magic of Tidying* (London: Vermilion, 2014).

10 Trilling, *Sincerity and Authenticity*, p. 4.

11 Beecham, Amy, '6 signs you're in a toxic relationship with yourself – and what you can do about it' [article], *Stylist* (2 July

2022), https://www.stylist.co.uk/health/mental-health/toxic-relationship-with-yourself-signs/678117. Accessed 28 July 2022.

12 Mull, Amanda, 'I Gooped Myself' [article], the *Atlantic* (26 August 2019), https://www.theatlantic.com/health/archive/2019/08/what-goop-really-sells-women/596773/. Accessed 17 July 2022.

13 Belluz, Julia, 'Goop was fined $145,000 for its claims about jade eggs for vaginas. It's still selling them' [article], *Vox* (6 September 2018), https://www.vox.com/2018/9/6/17826924/goop-yoni-egg-gwyneth-paltrow-settlement. Accessed 29 July 2022.

14 Price, Hannah, 'Belle Gibson: The influencer who lied about having cancer' [article], *BBC*, https://www.bbc.co.uk/bbcthree/article/b2538e04-87f5-4af5-bd6f-f6cf88b488c4. Accessed 29 July 2022.

15 Jones, Daisy, 'Why Everyone's Instagram Looks Ugly Now' [article], *Vice* (8 February 2022), https://www.vice.com/en/article/v7d79y/why-everyones-instagram-feed-looks-so-ugly-right-now. Accessed 17 July 2022.

16 Seal, Rebecca, 'Be bad, better – from anger to laziness, how to put your worst habits to good use' [article], *Guardian* (1 January 2022), https://www.theguardian.com/lifeandstyle/2022/jan/01/be-bad-better-from-anger-to-laziness-how-to-put-your-worst-habits-to-good-use?CMP=Share_iOSApp_Other. Accessed 29 July 2022.

17 Harris, Aisha, 'A History of Self-Care' [article], *Slate* (5 April 2017), http://www.slate.com/articles/arts/culturebox/2017/04/the_history_of_self_care.html?via=gdpr-consent&via=gdpr-consent. Accessed 29 July 2021.

18 Cited in Harris, 'A History of Self-Care'.

19 Nolan, Megan, *Acts of Desperation* (London: Jonathan Cape 2021).

20 Nolan, *Acts of Desperation*, p. 26.

21 Nolan, *Acts of Desperation*, p. 4.

22 Trilling, *Sincerity and Authenticity*, p. 73.

23 Tomalin, Clare, *Jane Austen: A Life* [ebook] (London: Penguin, 2012, first published 1997), p. 176.

24 Austen, *Sense and Sensibility*, p. 118.

25 Guignon, *On Being Authentic*, p. 36.

CONFESSION

1   Foucault, Michel, *The History of Sexuality Volume 1: The Will to Knowledge*, 5th edition (UK: Penguin 2020, first published 1976).

2   Foucault, *The Will to Knowledge*, p. 60.

3   Foucault, *The Will to Knowledge*, p. 59.

4   *Fleabag*, Season 2, Episode 2, BBC 1 (first aired 17 May 2019).

5   See Leszkiewicz, Anna, 'Sex, power and Fleabag' [article], *New Statesman* (8 April 2019), https://www.newstatesman.com/culture/2019/04/sex-power-and-fleabag. Accessed 11 May 2022.

6   Foucault, *The Will to Knowledge*, pp. 61–62.

7   Foucault, *The Will to Knowledge*, p. 62.

8   Taylor, *The Ethics of Authenticity*, p. 16.

9   Foucault, *The Will to Knowledge*, p. 65.

10 Foucault, *The Will to Knowledge*, p. 66.

11 Perls, Fritz, 'Four Lectures', in J. Fagan and I. L. Shepherd, eds., *Gestalt Therapy Now* (New York: Harper Colophon, 1970), pp. 20, 22, cited in Guignon, *On Being Authentic*, p. 2.

12 Freud, Sigmund, *The Ego and the Id*, Standard Edition, revised and edited by James Strachey, trans. Joan Riviere (New York: W. W. Norton, 1960, originally published in German 1923).

13 Concept first introduced in Freud, Sigmund, *The Interpretation of Dreams*, trans. A. A. Brill (Ware: Wordsworth Editions, 1997, first published 1899).

14 Freud, Sigmund, *Civilization and Its Discontents*, trans. James Strachey (New York: W.W. Norton, 1961), p. 12, cited in Guignon, *On Being Authentic*, p. 51.

15 See Guignon, *On Being Authentic*, pp. 49–50.

16 See Guignon, *On Being Authentic*, p. 50.

17 Miller, Alice, *The Drama of the Gifted Child: The Search for the True Self*, rev. edition (New York: Basic Books, 1997), cited in Guignon, *On Being Authentic*, pp. 45–46.

18 Phillips, Adam, *On Getting Better* (UK: Penguin Random House, 2021), p. 4.

19 Grosz, Stephen, *The Examined Life: How We Lose and Find Ourselves* (London: Chatto & Windus, 2013), pp. xi-xii.

20 Aristotle, *Nicomachean Ethics*, trans. T. Irwin (Indianapolis: Hackett, 1985), 1106a 21–4, cited in Guignon, *On Being Authentic*, p. 47.

21 *The Pervert's Guide to Ideology*, dir. Sophie Fiennes, written by Slavoj Žižek (Zeitgeist Films, 2012).

22 See 'Product', pp. 69–70, and Boyle, *Authenticity*, p. 162.

23 Michael James Schneider (@blcksmth), 'healing is sexy (quote by @wittyidiot, thanks to Travis Paulson for the assist and @matthewtylerpriestley for the photo edit)', Instagram (15 February 2021), https://www.instagram.com/p/CLUoNUih7-q/. Accessed 30 July 2022.

24 Greig, James, 'Why telling people to "go to therapy" isn't as enlightened as some think' [article], *i-D* (3 August 2021), https://i-d.vice.com/en_uk/article/5dbq4q/go-to-therapy-memes. Accessed 17 July 2022.

25 As cited in Tait, Amelia, 'Reality checks' [article], *Tortoise* (8 October 2019), https://www.tortoisemedia.com/2019/10/08/down-with-influencers-191008/. Accessed 30 July 2022.

26 Gevinson, Tavi, 'Who Would I Be Without Instagram?', *The Cut* (16 September 2019), https://www.thecut.com/2019/09/who-would-tavi-gevinson-be-without-instagram.html. Accessed 30 July 2022.

27 Beach, Natalie, 'I Was Caroline Calloway', *The Cut* (9 September 2019), https://www.thecut.com/2019/09/the-story-of-caroline-

calloway-and-her-ghostwriter-natalie.html. Accessed 30 July 2022.

28 'Tyson Fury says he wants to become a people's champion if he returns to boxing', *BBC Sport* (28 November 2017), https://www.bbc.co.uk/sport/boxing/42154202. Accessed 30 July 2022.

29 See Iovine, Anna, 'I Scammed Influencer Caroline Calloway at Her Event, The Scam' [article], *Vice* (6 August 2019), https://www.vice.com/en/article/pa7e9k/caroline-calloway-the-scam-event-essay. Accessed 30 July 2022.

30 Rousseau, *Confessions*, pp. 1–2.

31 Foucault, *The Will to Knowledge*, p. 59.

32 Hawthorne, Nathaniel, *The Scarlet Letter*, Ch. XXIV, 'Conclusion', as cited in Trilling, *Sincerity and Authenticity*, p. 5.

33 McCulloch, Gretchen, *Because Internet* (London: Harvill Secker, 2019), p. 105.

34 Foucault, *The Will to Knowledge*, p. 61.

ACKNOWLEDGEMENTS

Thank you, first and foremost, to Henry Rowley and Ortac Press, for taking on this project and bringing it to life. It has been the most amazing opportunity and I can't wait to see where the Press goes from here.

Thank you to my agent, Holly Faulks, for being a calm voice of reason throughout and putting up with my increasingly frantic emails – this could not have got out the door without you. Thank you to Jo Walker for the beautiful, perfect cover. Thank you to Richard Arcus and Tom Witcomb for your sharp eyes and for turning my garbled thoughts into sentences. And to Jaime Witcomb for making sure people read them.

Thank you so much to the friends and colleagues who have read extracts, recommended books and talked to me about these ideas: Sophie Eager, Florence Glanfield, Lola Seaton, and in particular Sarah Manavis, who has been my sounding board from day one.

Special thank you to my brother Sam, not just for being an endless source of wisdom on philosophy, and for spending time with a baby and a full-time job reading and talking to me about my work, but for helping me get a handle on the idea in the first place, in November 2019, over hipster flat whites in Durham. Thank you also for the perfect title, and for reminding me of the real meaning of essay (*essayer* – to try).

Thank you to Pippa Bailey and Peter Williams at the *New Statesman* for indulging my writerly moment, and to other kind and, frankly, intimidatingly intelligent colleagues, from whom I learn masses every day. Thank you to Polly and Jeremy Foster for letting me stay in beautiful Grosmont in much-needed solitude, and to Ruth and Mike Eyre not only for lending me your space on many occasions but for the constant supply of tea, beer and restorative rural vibes.

Thank you to the friends not yet mentioned who have provided support through this intense process, in particular Natasha Heliotis, Kim Guest, Aimee Bromwell, Caitlin Turner, Cressida Shaw, Hebe Foster, Ellie Caddick. Love you all. Thank you to my brother Tom for being a never-ending source of creative inspiration and showing me what constant hard work and determination looks like.

Thank you to Mum and Dad – for all your love and support, and for making me someone who wants to analyse, write and engage with the world. I couldn't have done this without you.

Thank you most of all to George Eyre – for your editing and encouragement, for your kindness, patience and love, and for making me laugh more than anyone I know. Without you I would not be – for the want of a better phrase – who I am.